1982

GEN
Poll
Mov

SO-AFY-106

3 0301 00080460 5

Moving On Up

❋

Ted Pollock

Moving On Up

HAWTHORN BOOKS
A division of Elsevier-Dutton
New York

LIBRARY
College of St. Francis
JOLIET, ILL.

For Barbara, again . . .

I should like to thank *Production* magazine for permission to use, in expanded form, some material that first appeared in the pages of several of its PLANBOOK issues; and the National Safety Council for allowing me to base chapter 9 on a special report originally written for it.

MOVING ON UP

Copyright © 1979 by Ted Pollock. Copyright under International and Pan-American Copyright Conventions. All rights reserved, including the right to reproduce this book or portions thereof in any form, except for the inclusion of brief quotations in a review. All inquiries should be addressed to Elsevier-Dutton, 2 Park Avenue, New York, New York 10016. This book was manufactured in the United States of America and published simultaneously in Canada by Prentice-Hall of Canada, Limited, 1870 Birchmount Road, Scarborough, Ontario.

Library of Congress Catalog Card Number: 78-71021
ISBN: 0-8015-4856-X

2 3 4 5 6 7 8 9 10 11 12 13 14 15 16 17 18 19 20

658.312
P782

Contents

	Introduction	vii
1.	How Do You Look to Your Boss?	1
2.	Plan Your Strategy	11
3.	Creating Your Own Public Relations Program	18
4.	Secrets of Self-Confidence	29
5.	Winning Habits: How to Cultivate Them	44
6.	Make the Time You Need	62
7.	How to Boost Your Personal Productivity	72
8.	Sharpen Your Communications Skills	92
9.	How to Teach	113
10.	How to Sell Your Ideas	123
11.	Managing Creativity	139
12.	Dealing with People—Creatively	150
13.	So You've Been Promoted—Now What?	166
	Index	173

101325

Introduction

Have you ever been inside the casino of a Las Vegas hotel? If not, let me describe it to you.

Cavernous, with lofty chandeliers that bathe it in a soft light, its extravagant architecture and decor are monuments to the art of industrial design. Splashing fountains, marble columns, murals of European cities and brocaded walls conspire to shut out any reminders of reality. The casino is alive twenty-four hours a day, seven days a week. The noise level ebbs and flows with the time of day, to be sure, but it is never totally quiet. At any given moment, somewhere the gears of a slot machine are whirring, chips are clicking genteelly against each other, roulette wheels are spinning, cards are being shuffled, the outcome of a dice roll is being announced, winning keno numbers are blinking alive on strategically located light boards. Shouts of triumph intermingle with groans of despair as individual fortunes rise and fall. Periodically an orchestra blares out the latest upbeat tune. Attractive cocktail waitresses in abbreviated costumes parade across plush carpeting on incredibly high heels to bring the gamblers any refreshments they desire—compliments of the house. The casino, in short, is a cunningly contrived pleasure palace dedicated to dreams. There are no clocks, no windows, no distractions from the business at hand. People are there for only one reason, to gamble, and the entire environment—gaudy, even vulgar, though it may be—is designed to make the pursuit of easy money as pleasurable an experience as possible.

If you want to take an elevator to your room from the lobby, you must walk through, or at least along the perimeter of, the casino. If you want to drop by the coffee shop or patronize a restaurant, you must walk through the casino. If you have a reservation for a show, you must line up in the casino. If you feel like a drink at the bar, you . . . but you get the idea.

Admittedly, the casinos of Las Vegas are the calculated creations of experienced designers, architects, psychologists, and interior decorators. Theirs is an irresistible allure that has helped nudge the state of Nevada's annual gaming take toward the $2 billion mark. And it continues to grow.

But their success cannot be explained solely in terms of the expert skills of their fabricators. No. The real reason behind the phenomenal success of the casinos as well as of the nation's racetracks, jai alai frontons, lotteries, bingo games, punchboards, numbers, raffles, and assorted sporting events (to the tune of an estimated $500 billion bet each year, according to gaming expert John Scarne) is one indisputable fact of human nature: Millions of men and women are eager to wager their money on spinning wheels, tumbling dice, the turn of a card, the call of a number, the speed of an animal, the skills of other human beings.

Yet, the overwhelming majority of these same men and women would never dream of betting on themselves!

They willingly gamble five, ten, twenty, fifty, a hundred dollars or more on something over which they have absolutely no control—but wager on a known quantity, themselves? Never!

Think about that.

Isn't it remarkable?

Yet the more you mingle with the people who have gone places in this world, the more aware you become of one particular denominator that they have in common. These people stick their neck out—all the time. They aren't afraid to take chances—on themselves. Afraid? They like nothing better than pitting their skills and resourcefulness against the challenge of a difficult opportunity. And it's easy to spot them, too, because you always find them at the top.

The timid soul, preoccupied with security-on-a-silver-platter, never knows the real security that comes from making good on the challenges you set for yourself. For the very act of daring to tackle the extra goal invariably summons the energy and resources needed to reach it.

It's clear where you stand. You've already proved that by buying, or contemplating buying, this book, and I congratulate you.

The question naturally arises, can a book really help you get ahead? *Really?* After all, if everybody purchased a copy of *Moving On Up* and it lived up to its promises, presumably there would be a sudden plethora of promotable men and women across the land. Clearly, the entire working population cannot be promoted.

Don't worry.

Not everyone who picks up this book is going to buy it.

Not everyone who buys it is going to read it.

Not everyone who reads it is going to practice the principles and techniques that it describes.

And not everyone who practices those principles and techniques is going to practice them correctly.

Consequently, if you do buy this book, read it, and take seriously what it professes to teach, you will, almost automatically, have outstripped most of your competition.

This is not to say that this book is a magical passport to career advancement. It is not. It is no substitute for knowledge, initiative, intelligence, perseverance, ambition, curiosity, good judgement, the ability to solve problems, or the practice of good human relations.

What this book *can* do is sensitize you to the traits and skills that getting ahead requires, help you fill in the gaps in your personal arsenal of qualifications, sharpen those you already possess, and maximize the rewards that ought to accrue to you for possessing—and using—them.

In short, if you are willing to bet on yourself, *Moving On Up* will help you load the dice in your favor . . . legally.

No gambler could ask for more.

Moving On Up

How Do You Look to Your Boss?

You know your job; you like what you do; you get along with your fellow employees. You're ambitious. Your company is growing. Your prospects look very good indeed.

Don't kid yourself.

Most people do their work well. They, too, are conscientious, competent, cooperative. In the world of business, being good at what you do is frequently not enough to make you stand out from the crowd. In order to be appreciated and rewarded, you must also be *perceived* as being good and deserving of advancement.

Are you? Whether you are relatively new on the job or an old hand, a professional or in middle management, you have a constituency of one whom you must satisfy and, ultimately, impress if you are to get ahead— your boss. Is he aware of your abilities, aspirations, and potential? Maybe, maybe not. If he isn't, you may be missing out on salary increases, opportunities to assume additional responsibilities, promotions.

It may be helpful, therefore, to take stock of your image right now. By determining as frankly and fully as possible the qualities and skills that your name conjures up in your boss's mind, you can go a long way toward pinpointing those areas in which you already excel as well as those in which you ought to apply additional effort. What follows is an exhaustive questionnaire; your candid and considered answers should give you a running start toward new self-knowledge.

1. What is your first reaction upon being handed an assignment different from anything you've done before—apprehension? "All-in-a-day's-work"? Enthusiastic anticipation?

2. Are you an adaptable person, able to assimilate new experiences, or do you tend to be thrown off center by the unfamiliar and the untried?

3. Are you generally confident about your ability to adapt to new circumstances?

4. Do you tend to assume that any change is bound to be a change for the worse?

5. Are you conscious of a more or less habitual feeling of anxiety and insecurity?

6. Do you actively seek out new responsibilities?

7. Do you keep up with developments in your field?

8. When did you last add to your job skills or knowledge? Explain.

9. Specifically, what have you done to prepare yourself for your next step upward?

10. Are you well organized? Do you have the habit of getting things done promptly and getting them out of the way, or do you tend to let them pile up until their sheer number is discouraging?

11. Was everything under control when you last took a vacation, or did you return to face confusion, dissatisfied superiors, a crisis or two?

12. Do you keep pretty much on top of your paper work?

13. When things are going exceptionally well, do you take advantage of the psychological boost by tackling other tough chores, or do you bask in your accomplishment and ease up for the rest of the day or week?

14. Are the meetings you attend always necessary? Always productive? Always the kind you couldn't afford to miss?

15. Do you use priorities in your planning, establishing what has to be done immediately, what decisions need to be made first, which can be deferred, which require additional information?

16. Do you anticipate what you will need, how long it will take, whose help you can call on before you undertake an assignment?

17. Do you sit down periodically for some serious self-examination, evaluating your own performance, identifying weaknesses, setting personal achievement goals?

18. Name two such goals that you have reached and two that remain to be realized.

19. Do you express yourself clearly? Do others immediately understand what you say and write?

20. Are you dissatisfied with your correspondence until it says precisely what you want it to say, no more and no less?

21. Do you favor short, direct words over multisyllabic expressions?

22. Do you present your ideas clearly, with facts in a logical sequence to back them up?

23. Are you good on your feet, in front of an audience, or are you a nervous and inept speaker?

24. Are you at ease before your company's high-level executives or do you feel distinctly uncomfortable dealing directly with the brass?

25. Are you a convincing communicator? Can you persuade others to agree with your viewpoint?

26. Are you a tactful person? Can you persuade people to change their ways and do things differently without hurting their feelings?

27. Do you ever use humor effectively in your work relationships?

28. Do you speak clearly, without slurring or mispronouncing words? Do you speak too fast or too slowly for comprehension?

29. Do you view problems as barriers to getting your work done or, more realistically, as *part* of the work for which you are responsible?

30. Do you assign reasonable priorities to your problems, or do you fall into the trap of considering every problem a crisis of the same magnitude?

31. When headlong assault on a problem proves ineffective, do you ever try to outflank it with a completely fresh approach?

32. Do you tackle a problem as soon as you are aware of its existence, or do you tend to postpone it as long as possible in the hope that it will somehow take care of itself?

33. Do you panic under pressure, and consequently reach for any solution? Or do you realize that answers may not come for a while, thus remaining capable of doing other work while the problem simmers on a back burner in your brain?

34. When faced with a problem, do you try to isolate the key element, on the supposition that if you can crack it, everything else will fall into place?

35. When a solution to a problem doesn't work out, do you discard it entirely, or do you consider what parts of it may be salvaged, modified, or amended?

36. Are *you* ever the problem—through indecision, poor communication, insufficient research, lack of planning, failure to assign enough people to a job, and so on?

37. Do you ever reach across functional lines to tap the minds of others who may be able to view your problem from a fresh perspective?

38. Do you use the telephone effectively in your problem solving, for example, for quick consultations with others, for contacting libraries or private agencies for information not readily available on your own premises, for tracking down data?

39. Are you stubborn in the best sense of the word, unwilling to give up when something has you stymied?

40. When a problem has you baffled, do you recognize that frustration is a part of the problem-solving process, or do you take your frustrations out on those around you?

41. Do you maintain an up-to-date collection of books and articles that you find especially stimulating or that apply specifically to your job and the kinds of problems you are apt to encounter?

42. Confronted by an unfamiliar problem, do you examine it for familiar elements so that you may bring into play past experiences, knowledge, and ideas that can start you on the road to a solution?

43. What is your department's main problem? What are you doing to help solve it?

44. When you are in contact with others in your company or industry, do you keep alert to any new approaches they may be using in their jobs, with a view toward adapting them to your own needs?

45. Do you view your job primarily as a creative one or as a fairly cut-and-dried proposition that simply requires a certain amount of output?

46. Do ideas excite you?

47. Do you have confidence in your own ideas? Does it bother you when others denigrate your ideas? Or, once convinced that you are right, do you stick to your guns?

48. When you propose an idea, are you prepared to answer possible objections to it convincingly? In other words, have you thought your idea out in detail before presenting it?

49. Do you read widely, outside your own specialty?

50. When you come across a clever idea in a field other than your own—in your reading, for instance—do you ask yourself, "How can I use this?"

51. Are you receptive to and tolerant of new ideas, no matter what their source?

52. Do you ever challenge company policies or methods?

53. Have you originated any new projects that had substantive value for your department or company?

54. Have you devised any new work methods or procedures that reduce waste, save time, or conserve material for your company?

55. Do you manage to structure yourself some time during your workday for the express purpose of doing some hard thinking?

56. Do you reserve judgment while creating, concentrating on quantity and variety rather than on quality?

57. Have you identified the people in your company whose knowledge and advice can be drawn upon from time to time to prime the pumps of your own thinking?

58. Do you ever doodle your way to creativity by "playing" on paper with the factors involved in a problem?

59. Are you aware of any biases, preconceived notions, or personal flaws that inhibit your creativity, for example, discounting the abilities of others, assuming that certain facts are unobtainable, a predisposition toward giving up too soon? If you are aware of them, do you consciously ward them off while in the throes of creativity?

60. Would you say that you practice effective human relations?

61. If you are a manager, do your people know what is expected of them at all times?

62. Have you made it clear to them that you are all on the same team and that they can come to you with questions and problems without risking your displeasure?

63. Do you show respect for their knowledge and, on occasion, defer to their expertise, even when you don't agree with them?

64. Can you identify your best performer?

65. What can your other people learn from him or her that might help them upgrade their own performances?

66. What is this top performer's career goal? And what are you doing to help him or her realize it?

67. Who is your least effective employee?

68. In what areas is he or she weakest? What are you doing to strengthen this weakness?

69. Can you identify the chief nonbusiness interests of each person who works for you?

70. Without prying, do you have a pretty clear idea of any outside problems that may be adversely affecting the performance of your people (for example, ill health, alcoholism, compulsive gambling, financial setbacks)?

71. Can you identify the motivational hot button of each employee, that is, the single most important factor that drives him or her (desire to excel, need for approval, competitive spirit, etc.)?

72. Do you take these into consideration when giving assignments, assessing performance, appraising overall effectiveness?

73. Can you predict with a fair degree of accuracy how each of your people will react to criticism? A setback? An unfamiliar assignment? A change in environment?

74. Who, among your people, are the challenge meeters, that is, the men and women who tackle tough assignments with relish because they view them as opportunities to prove themselves?

75. Are these employees given the kind of jobs that require innovative thinking, perseverance, and plain hard work?

76. Realizing that people bridle at being policed but like to know that their manager is interested in their progress, do you follow up and follow through on projects once they are launched?

77. Are any of your people getting more than their fair share of work?

78. By the same token, is anyone being underemployed?

79. How would you characterize morale among the people reporting to you: excellent, good, or poor?

80. Are your people generally satisfied with the way you handle grievances?

81. If not, what do they object to? Is their objection justified?

82. Have any of your people ever had reason—real or imaginary—to complain to your boss about your treatment of them?

83. What sort of image do you project to your people—tough, arbitrary, inconsistent, demanding but fair, incompetent, what?

84. Do your people know you not just as a boss, but as a human being, that is, do they know your outside interests, enthusiasms, hobbies, and so on?

85. How do your people get along with one another? Do they cooperate in a team spirit? Compete in a healthy way? Willingly pitch in on projects when they are needed? Or do they generally go their separate ways, avoiding involvement with each other?

86. Is absenteeism or chronic lateness a problem?

87. If they are, have you investigated the possibility that they may be symptomatic of a deeper problem?

88. Do you arrange for your people to have some solitude occasionally, just to do creative thinking?

89. Do you think that your people get a sense of contributing to the success of your department, function, or company?

90. Whenever possible, do you give them an opportunity to participate in decisions?

91. Do you take each employee's capabilities into consideration, then give him assignments that challenge and "stretch" him?

92. Are your work assignments effective? That is, do you give your people meaningful jobs from the successful completion of which they derive personal satisfaction?

93. Within the limits possible, do you allow your people freedom to do things *their* way?

94. Do you make a practice of varying jobs so that boredom has no chance to set in? For instance, do you alternate "dry" assignments with those requiring some creativity, deskwork with legwork, work done alone with work done with others?

95. Have you sat down at least once with each employee during the past year and had a frank exchange of views about his or her performance and progress?

96. Do you keep informed on how your people are thinking and feeling by chatting with them on an informal basis now and then?

97. Could you describe the ambitions of each of your people, their short- and long-range goals?

98. Do you encourage them to express their ideas and opinions rather than being mere mouthpieces for your decisions?

99. Do you really listen to them? That is, does what they say ever modify your own ideas or actions?

100. Do you keep your people informed of changes in company policies and procedures as well as all other matters affecting their work?

101. Do you keep informed about developments that affect your department, company, industry?

102. Do you inform higher levels of management of your people's accomplishments?

103. When you make a decision, do you explain the reasoning behind it?

104. Are you accessible when your people need to see you?

105. When was the last time you held a meeting with your people?

106. Are such meetings conducted on a regular basis?

107. Do your meetings tend to be informal, offering your people a chance to express their views openly? Or are they highly formal and a bit stiff?

108. In between meetings, do you maintain regular two-way communications with each of your people?

109. Have you ever asked them if they find your meetings worthwhile?

110. Do your people generally come to you when they want information or do they seek it elsewhere?

111. Do you clearly communicate to them what you want done, why they should do it, and when you want it finished?

112. Do you and your subordinates agree on what results are expected of them?

113. Do you agree on measures of performance?

114. Is accountability fixed for each delegated responsibility? Is your follow-up in this area adequate?

115. Do you ever usurp the prerogatives of subordinates by making decisions that are rightfully part of their jobs?

116. Do you do things your subordinates should do? Why?

117. How could you best improve your delegation of responsibility?

118. If you were incapacitated for three months, who could take your place?

119. Have you been grooming your own successor so that, if a bigger job suddenly became available, you could leave your current position without disrupting the operations of your department?

120. Are you courteous to your people?

121. Would you say you have their respect?

122. Of what recent achievement are you proudest? Is your boss aware of it?

123. Have you ever saved your boss from making a serious mistake?

124. When was the last time he singled you out for praise? Gave you a raise?

125. To your knowledge, has *his* boss ever spoken well of you to him?

126. Do you think your boss views you as a comer? Why?

127. What would you say he considers to be your single greatest strength? Weakness? Is his assessment justified?

128. When there is a crisis in your department, does he tend to call on you for help?

129. Has he seen you perform well under pressure?

130. Does he keep his supervision of you to a minimum, or does he continually check on your progress?

131. Has he delegated any responsibility to you that includes the spending of significant amounts of money?

132. Has he ever had occasion to dress you down? Was it warranted?

133. Is he generally receptive to your ideas?

134. Does he ask you to represent him at meetings?

135. When he must be out of the office for any extended length of time, does he ever have you sit in for him?

136. Does he have faith in your ability to handle people?

137. Is he aware of your background? Experience? Interests? Ambitions?

138. Has he ever discussed your future with you on optimistic terms?

139. Has he ever nominated you for advanced training, either inside or outside your company?

140. If he were asked to rank the people who report to him according to merit, where do you think he would place you?

141. Would you say he trusts your judgment? Explain.

142. Has he gradually added to your responsibilities since you joined his department?

143. Has he ever appointed you to a task force?

144. Are you ever asked to head a project?

145. Do you think your boss views you as a person who plans his work and is always in control of it or as one who often fights losing battles with deadlines?

146. Do you enjoy a reputation for excellence with him? Does he tend to assume that if he gives you an assignment, it will be carried out efficiently and intelligently?

147. Think carefully. In view of your answers to the foregoing questions, if you had to characterize your boss's perception of you in a single paragraph, what would you say?

No boss walks around continually assessing his people, of course. He's too busy for that. But he does see you in action daily. If only subliminally, his thoughts dart to his people from time to time, weighing merits, judging capabilities, comparing performances, tagging them with one label or another—"immature," "dependable," "uncooperative," "bright," "lazy," "high potential," "a loser," "a leader." And when he has time to review the day's activities or when he is specifically asked to recommend someone for a newly available job, he will mentally summon up his overall impressions of you and your colleagues. Needless to say, the conclusions to which he comes can have a powerful effect on your future.

Fortunately, as we shall see, there are ways and means at your disposal to influence his conclusions and, therefore, to exert a large measure of control over your own professional destiny.

2

Plan Your Strategy

Armed with an objective view of your assets and liabilities, you are ready to plan your strategy for getting ahead. There is really no secret about the methodology to be used here. You go about it very much as if you were planning a physical move. If you were considering changing your place of residence, you would take certain commonsense precautions before signing any papers and committing yourself. You would make sure the move was really what you wanted. Specifically, you would scout the neighborhood to determine the availability of public transportation and the proximity of stores; you would inquire into the quality of the school system and the property tax structure. You would certainly examine the foundation of the house for soundness, its basement for dryness, the land it stood on for adequate drainage. And you would scrutinize the roof, the fireplace, the heating system, and a score of other items that make for comfortable, trouble-free housing.

Why do anything less for the job you've leveled your sights on? It's where you may very well spend the next five years or more of your life.

The opportunities are there, perhaps more than ever before. As the competition among companies, both national and international, intensifies, the demand for talented, experienced managers is rising exponentially. The "whiz kids" of only a few years ago have fallen into disrepute as many of their decisions have cost their companies money, as well as the competitive edge they once enjoyed. The result is a new appreciation of the older, more basic virtues: knowledge, experience, and an understanding of how a business works.

Where are these management paragons to be found? Increasingly, business is turning to its own first- and second-line managers to fill the gaps, providing these junior executives can prove themselves ready and willing to move up.

Are you?

Could you, if called upon, take the reins from your boss? Do you have

a grasp of the business as a whole? Do you have the background, temperament, and confidence to make the hard decisions that are often necessary?

If you don't, it's time you started training yourself so that when
opportunity knocks, you can open the door. The suggestions that follow
will help you prepare yourself for that upward move.

Analyze the Job You Want

Start at the beginning by identifying as precisely as possible the position you're aiming for. Maybe it's heading the Engineering Department
or moving up in Personnel or assuming more responsibility in Operations.
Whatever it is, know what it is you want.

When you do, analyze the requirements of the job. If your boss is
moving up and you are eyeing his job, for example, what is his routine?
What is he responsible for? To whom does he report? What sort of
decisions must he make? Who are the people with whom he ordinarily
deals? What special knowledge or training does his position require (for
example, an advanced degree in business administration, hands-on
experience with certain machinery, a knowledge of data processing,
purchasing know-how, familiarity with the performance of competitive
products, a thorough background in international finance)?

Without hounding him, notice how your boss spends a typical
workday. Does he attend many meetings? If he does, the ability to communicate effectively may be especially important in his position. Do his
responsibilities bring him into frequent contact with the top brass? Poise
and social know-how may be important aspects of his work. Does
paperwork take up a lot of his time? The job may require a lot of
planning, orderliness, the ability to anticipate needs. Do his responsibilities demand much fieldwork? Travel may be a requisite of his job. Does
he keep long hours? The job may call for some family sacrifices.

In particular, pay attention to his relationships with those under him.
Has he come to rely on them for the routine parts of his responsibilities,
or is he saddled with a lot of details himself? As one of the people
reporting to him, how much freedom do you enjoy? From informal
contacts with your own peers, how does he rate as a boss? Any gripes
about how he runs his shop? Treats his people? Gets things done? In his
shoes, what would *you* do differently? What about his attitude? Does he

listen to his people? Is he temperamental? Fair? A perfectionist? What pressures does he work under?

Once you've analyzed the job, its responsibilities, and the man himself, take stock of yourself. How do you measure up? Do your experience, training, and temperament suit you to the job? What gaps in your knowledge or abilities can you identify?

If you've ever taken over your boss's job on a temporary basis—when he was on vacation, for example—how did you perform? Did things run relatively smoothly? Were there any emergencies with which you could not cope? Did you feel comfortable? What parts of the job did you find most congenial? Most important, in what part of the job were you ill at ease? Once you pinpoint your strengths and weaknesses, write them down. Divide a sheet of paper into two columns, one for strengths, the other for weaknesses; then see where you stand.

If, for example, you currently supervise two engineers and have set your sights on being put in charge of the entire department, your list might look something like this:

Strengths	Weaknesses
Engineering degree	Never dealt directly with customers
Seven years in department	Limited contacts with other departments
Three years of supervisory experience	Restricted knowledge of product line
Proven ability to bring out the best in others	No experience with budgets
Familiarity with company goals	Little experience in originating ideas

Eliminate Your Weaknesses

The next step, obviously, is to work on your weaknesses until they qualify as strengths.

Take our engineer supervisor. Recognizing that he lacks experience in dealing with customers, what might he do to fill in the gaps? He could ask his boss about what goes on at such meetings. He might volunteer to accompany his boss to his next business meeting, if only as an observer. Perhaps he could review pertinent correspondence in order to get the feel of working with a customer—the questions that arise, the problems that must be ironed out, the compromises that have to be made.

Or consider his limited contacts with other departments. The obvious remedy is to take measures to increase his exposure to them. One strategy might be as elementary as making it his business to lunch with someone from a different department each day. People generally like to talk about what they do and how their jobs fit into the bigger picture. Informal visits to other departments, properly timed, can be eye-openers, as can attendance at various presentations. And don't overlook the possibility of telephoning colleagues in other departments to ask them for help or information.

To counteract his lack of knowledge of the product line, he might study some company catalogs and reprints of advertisements. A heart-to-heart talk with some of the company's sales representatives could be extremely helpful. A visit to a trade show could provide insights into the entire industry.

No experience with budgets? Our engineer supervisor can ask his boss questions or perhaps get permission to study the department's budget. Many companies conduct special courses for their first-line managers covering such subjects. Getting a good grounding in planning expenditures might be as easy as calling up the Accounting Department and borrowing some manuals.

As for our engineer's "little experience in originating ideas," the way to become an idea person is through practice. He might start displaying some initiative on the job, if he hasn't already done so, by submitting ideas, modifications of existing ones, or criticisms of accepted ones. He could start studying customers' needs more carefully, with a view toward filling them in innovative ways.

In short, weaknesses can be transformed into strengths by identifying them; making an effort to overcome them; and then overcompensating by turning them into strengths (see chapter 4).

Learn All You Can

No matter how long you've been in your present job, it is doubtful that you know everything there is to know about it. What has been going on in your field? What are the long-range results of the research and development in your industry apt to be?

It might pay to investigate the educational opportunities offered by your company, as well as by your local university or community college. Possibilities range from courses in basic business practices to ones in advanced psychology.

Or take the broader area of management, where things are continually changing. There is much to be learned here. One simple example: As mandatory retirement ages are raised and inflation continues, more people are working longer. As these older workers—knowledgeable, experienced, with certain earned prerogatives like long vacations—increase in number, they are altering many familiar business practices. To what incentives are they most likely to respond? Suppose a physical change like failing eyesight makes it impracticable for a senior worker to continue at his old job? What are your viable options as a manager? How do you criticize or discipline someone who may be old enough to be your father and who has been doing his job considerably longer than you? Little in a manager's past experience is geared to prepare him for dealing with this new phenomenon. In order to get the answers he needs, he must be *au courant* with the news, with federal and state legislation, with his firm's policies, with what other companies are doing, with how senior workers feel. And he must be willing to learn and change with the times.

Then there is knowledge of your company to consider. What is its history? How did it get where it is today? For what innovations is it responsible? What about its products? What manufacturing processes do the raw materials go through? What inspection and quality-control methods do your manufacturing plants utilize to assure product excellence? What's your company's record as far as pollution control is concerned? Some ways to find out the facts: Tour your firm's factories; try out its products if possible.

The best way to learn, in short, is to approach everything with an inquiring mind and ask questions. We shall examine the learning process in more detail later.

Make Sure You Want It

Once you have some idea of what your boss does, how he does it, the demands of his job and whether or not you are qualified to move up, you should pose this all-important question to yourself: Do you really want the job?

There is no culpability or shame in deciding that it's not for you. Success means different things to different people. More aware of the world outside their narrow business focus than their predecessors have been, some men and women are taking a hard look at what they really want out of life. Sometimes it isn't what they used to think it was.

Many still want to scale the heady summit of power and prestige. But others prefer to stay where they are, doing familiar work with relatively narrow responsibilities, and having time for family, friends, and outside interests.

Stepping up only to discover that it isn't for you can be traumatic. So before you reach for the brass ring of promotion, it's a good idea to examine it carefully with a view toward determining whether it is truly what you want—and need—at this stage of your life.

To determine whether that promotion is the chance of a lifetime or an invitation to personal disaster, enter into "executive session" with yourself and do some hard thinking. For example, are you willing to pay the price in hard work and loss of leisure time that promotion often exacts? Will you resent having less time to devote to family and friends? Since the bigger the job, the greater the chance of exposure, are you prepared to accept the consequences if you are ever guilty of a costly mistake? Is the job a stepping-stone to still bigger things or a dead end with no future beyond it? These are important considerations, and your answers will depend on your own life situation, your immediate aspirations, your long-term goals.

Then there are those questions that depend on your personality and sense of values. How important is money to you? Do you place a high value on professional success? Are you likely to feel comfortable intellectually and socially with your new colleagues? If the new position involves intense pressures, can you cope with the accompanying nervous strain?

A promotion at this point in your life may be the very best thing that could possibly happen to you. But, on the other hand, it could be the wrong move at the wrong time. You are the only one who can decide.

In a nutshell: Be very sure you want it.

Groom Your Own Successor

If you decide that you do indeed want that promotion, make sure you can vacate your present position without penalty. One of the most overlooked stumbling blocks to promotion is the lack of a suitable successor to the promoted man. If *your* job can't be filled, you may find yourself stuck with it by default.

Can you identify your own successor? If you can, fine. But if you can't, it may be time to give him or her some thought.

Obviously, you want someone who, above all, knows his job and how to do it. In addition, he ought to display those characteristics important to an effective employee: resourcefulness, flexibility, self-confidence, an ability to work with and through others.

Once you spot him, give him assignments to complete, problems to solve, and decisions to make that will help him mature on the job. Coach him in those areas where he is weakest. Expose him, as rapidly as he can digest them, to the day-to-day problems of your job. If possible, give him enough autonomy to make his own mistakes. If he has what you think he has, he will learn from them.

Remember that one of the criteria of your own ability as a manager is the number of people you succeed in training for bigger and better things. Helping others get ahead is the hallmark of the manager destined for advancement himself.

3

Creating Your Own
Public Relations Program

When Phineas Taylor Barnum was thirty-one, a husband, a father—and broke—he decided to buy a down-at-the-heels museum in New York City for $15,000. Amidst the derision of friends, be bought Scudder's American Museum on credit and, drawing on his own impressive array of talents, turned it into a money maker in less than a year.

Those talents were multitudinous. By his thirtieth birthday Barnum had clerked in a number of stores, successfully run a series of lotteries, founded and edited a weekly newspaper, toured the South as an itinerant showman with a mediocre circus, sold Bibles door-to-door, manufactured shoe polish, and written advertising copy for a New York theater.

Like most successful men, Barnum learned something from everything he did. From dealing with people across a counter, he mastered the principles of salesmanship. From running lotteries, he developed a special appreciation of the value of advertising. His experience as an editor and copywriter gave him a deep respect for the magic of the written word.

But most important was what his career as a showman taught him. "The greatest lesson I ever learned," he reminisced in later life, "was that everything depended on getting people to think and talk and become curious and excited about you." Upon that single insight was built one of America's most colorful and successful careers.

The Importance of Recognition

Biographers and researchers make an endless game of trying to narrow down and single out the elements uniquely present in the lives of those who have reached the peak of their profession. These "what-it-takes-to-be-successful" lists are anything but unanimous. The more closely you examine each requisite, the more exceptions come to mind. One cites "a high degree of self-discipline" as a trait universally shared by the successful. But you need only think of Diamond Jim Brady, who would himself

18

have been the last to claim this virtue, or Bet-A-Million Gates, with his unbridled temper and wild contempt for discipline.

Is hard work the key to success? As valid as it may sound, not even this conventional wisdom stands up under scrutiny. Socrates drove poor old Xanthippe to pot-throwing fury with his loafing, irresponsible ways. And Alexander Graham Bell was an easygoing dreamer who puttered his way into history.

In all the attempts to identify the basic building blocks of success, the list grows longer and longer. But three essential ingredients survive all the tests and defy exception:

- Ability. There has never been a truly successful person who could not do at least one thing considerably better than most people.
- Opportunity. The availability of a showcase for that ability is an indisputable prerequisite for success.
- Recognition. The acknowledgment of that ability by a third party of some importance completes the success equation.

Although ability and opportunity seem obvious, many overlook the centrality of recognition in success. Would Shakespeare be a great dramatist if no one read his plays? Would Rembrandt be a great artist if no one looked at his paintings? Of course not.

Similarly, your own talents will do you little good, aside from self-satisfaction, unless they are recognized by someone else.

Can you lead others? You may never get the chance if your boss is unaware of your ability. Are you exceptionally proficient at what you do? Unless the people up front know that you are, your proficiency will not do your career much good. Do you deserve to be promoted? Your chances are slim unless somebody in authority recognizes your merit.

Although we have been speaking of ability, opportunity, and recognition as if that were their immutable order, in reality success is more often the result of this sequence: ability, recognition, opportunity. For, with few exceptions, we must depend on others to provide the showcase for our talent. Thus, recognition occupies a pivotal position in your drive to get ahead.

Recognition is unique in another way, too. Whereas we are all limited in our abilities by heredity and training and cannot always find the opportunities best suited to our talents, we can take concrete, specific action to assure being noticed.

That's the exciting, promising thing about recognition, about creating the right image for yourself: It is the one success factor that you can control. The amount and quality of the notice that you get is entirely up to you.

Your Public

Each of us plays to a special public. A sales rep wants to be recognized by potential customers, purchasing agents, secretaries, receptionists, and perhaps one or two vice-presidents. An actor aims at impressing play-wrights, producers, directors, talent scouts, and columnists. After giving it some thought, you may decide that your own public consists of your boss, your boss's boss, and the president of your division.

Very well. Somehow, you must make them aware of your existence. Over a period of time, they must come to appreciate the distinctive pluses that make up your unique personality, ability, and potential— all those things, over and above the standard qualities shared by all good workers, that make you a particularly desirable and promotable employee.

How do you do that?

As we will see in the following pages, the answer is no great secret. You do that by doing the things that people have always done to get ahead. In the process, you create a highly positive image of yourself. Call it public relations. Call it investing in your future. Whatever its name, it makes good sense.

Know Your Job

A comer is identified on the basis of past performance. Performance is action; but behind action lies attitude because your attitude toward your job vitally affects the way you perform. Behind attitude lies appreciation—the value you set on your job. If you think it mean and unimportant, you will give it only half your mind and strength. If you see it in terms of the contribution it makes to the whole work of your team or company, you will give it all you have.

So know your job, not only in the sense of knowing how to do it but also in the sense of knowing what it means to the bigger operation of which it is a part. A riveter on an airplane assembly line helps keep his country strong, makes it possible for businessmen to carry on their work, speeds men and women to their loved ones. A production worker in a computer plant may be turning out a crucial link in the national space effort. A sales representative helps keep the wheels of industry spinning. There never was a successful employee who did not have the ability to see an operation in its entirety and appreciate the essential part his own work had in making it complete.

Look for Better Methods

One decisive characteristic of a true "promotable" is that he or she is always on the hunt for ways to get the job done more effectively, not just for the sake of promotion but for the sheer joy of doing the job as well as it can possibly be done. Creative ideas are the foundation of progress. Imagination is a sign and assurance of ability. American industrial history is full of examples of men and women who found better ways to do things and thereby launched distinguished careers.

Case in point: A young railway mail clerk, like many hundreds of others, is distributing mail by primitive methods. Letters are sorted and routed largely by guesswork. Many are needlessly delayed for days, even weeks. But this clerk starts thinking. He works out a map or connecting routes and tacks it up in the car. He develops a new system of assembling mail for various points. The clerk's name is Theodore Vail. This simple act is one of the big events of his career. His charts and schemes attract notice. Shortly thereafter he is promoted. Five years later he is assistant superintendant of railroad mail service, soon to be general superintendant, and already on his way to becoming head of the American Telephone and Telegraph Company.

To do more than is expected, to take extra care, to assume extra responsibility, to look beyond the day's work—these are the surefire avenues to gaining the attention of superiors.

It was largely through putting in that "extra lick" that Eugene Grace rose in eight years from switching engines to millionairedom and the presidency of Bethlehem Steel.

Charles Markham, who went on to become chairman of the Illinois Central Railroad, began his climb one day when he was sweeping a station platform in blue shirt and overalls. Some officials observed the way he went about it. One of them said later that he handled his job "like a brisk piece of engineering."

"The man who attracts attention," Charles Schwab of Bethlehem Steel said, "is the man who is thinking all the time and expressing himself in little ways . . . not the man who tries to dazzle his employer by doing the theatrical, the spectacular." He mentions one employee "in the works" who was promoted merely because, when his shift went off duty, he always stayed "until he had talked over the day's problems with his successor." His genuine interest in his job impressed his superiors.

Simply saving an employer's time can often set a person apart from others. Marcus Bell, for example, who rose rapidly and became vice-president of the Rock Island Railroad as a very young man, attributed his success partially to this fact: When he received an order, he did not lean on his boss in carrying it out. No matter how complicated the order might be, he always took care *not* to ask how to execute it.

The president of a bank with four thousand employees once described his problem in finding men prepared to bear greater responsibility. Spreading his hands apart on the top of his desk, he said, "Suppose I had a thousand men here standing in line with a commander in front of them. To the commander they all look alike. He cannot judge them as individuals. Only if certain of them step forward can they become marked men. I am always on the lookout for someone to step forward from among the employees in this bank. If these men only knew that their greatest problem is getting the attention of the boss. Initiative and courage are required to do something different—something that has not been ordered."

Sometimes, whether it's going beyond the call of duty to find a better way or coming up with an unorthodox solution to a problem, it's worth running risks in order to step forward from the ranks.

Be a Maverick

The navy can't shoot for beans! That's the gist of a remarkable letter that a young lieutenant once sent to President Theodore Roosevelt.

In writing it he broke all the rules, ripped through miles of red tape, and went directly over the heads of his commanding officers and of the secretary of the Navy, all of whom had declined to listen to his ideas. Now William Sowden Sims, at the risk of punishment—even disgrace—was placing his plans before the president himself.

This was the first important step in the brilliant career of Admiral Sims, commander of the U.S. fleet in European waters during World War I, who was called "the ablest figure of his generation in the sea establishment."

The immediate result was that five battleships of the Atlantic squadron were placed at the disposal of this "upstart" lieutenant. Next, he himself was promoted to the rank of commander and made inspector of target practice.

Sims had sound ideas, and he demonstrated them. But equally important, he had the courage to smash through red tape. By this one act, he won the attention he deserved, stepped forward from the crowd and laid the groundwork of his reputation.

Admittedly, this can sometimes be a dangerous strategy. In using it, you must be sure that you can meet a real need. But once you are convinced that you can deliver, the risk is often richly repaid.

Andrew Carnegie often promoted people merely because they used common sense in breaking some iron-clad rule. "If a man can't see the need for breaking rules," he explained, "I recognize that he has reached the limit of his ability."

There are necessary exceptions to every rule in a business. And in most businesses, certain rules and customs exist that have long ceased to serve any useful purpose. All too many men adhere to them merely because to do so is safe and easy. Yet to challenge such sacred cows is often a simple way to serve the employer's best interests and to gain recognition. Obedience and discipline are essential in every organization, certainly. An employee must obey orders, sometimes blindly. But when something is going wrong, the able employee who wants to get ahead starts outthinking his job.

Accept Criticism Graciously

Thomas Carlyle once declared that if any poet could be "killed off by one critique" or many, the sooner he was so dispatched, the better. What he said certainly applies to employees. If a person cannot take criticism, he or she will never advance up the executive ladder. You may become a "boss," a "dictator," a "little Napoleon," but you will never be a top executive.

It is in the nature of people to criticize each other's work; and it is in the nature of a sensible people to listen to criticism of their work, sifting the valid from the superficial and incorporating that which is true into their future behavior and performance.

When your superior criticizes you, listen carefully. He may say something from which you can learn.

On the other hand, he may be opening the way to finding out whether you really know what you are doing and why you are doing it the way you do. Offer your countersuggestions. There is no better way in the world to clarify your own thinking and confidence than to talk your ideas and practices out in the presence of a challenging person.

Either way—whether you listen and learn or successfully defend yourself against criticism—you win; for in the process you will be recognized as a person who thinks things through and therefore knows what he is doing.

Learn to Disagree—Agreeably

Sometimes *you* must be the critic. A colleague opposes an idea of yours that you are convinced is good . . . your boss is wrong, and you *know* it . . . a customer is heading toward disaster, and you feel it is your duty to dissuade him. What can you do?

You will never be far off the mark if you do what you believe is right. But since it is often easier to convince another person with tact than with bull-headed opposition, you must approach the situation in such a way as to turn a potential argument into a constructive discussion. In short, you must learn to disagree agreeably. Among the best methods of defusing potentially explosive confrontations are these.

Be Pleasant. This doesn't mean putting on an artificial smile that masks insincerity. A pleasant, congenial manner starts inside. A genuine liking for and appreciation of others requires making an honest effort to understand them and their ideas.

Listen Carefully. What you hear affects your reply. Too often we are so busy planning our answers that we don't listen. If you do this, you may lose the real meaning or fail to differentiate between fact and opinion. As a result, you may accuse the other person wrongly or, at the very least, display a lack of understanding of the issue involved.

Avoid Words that Emphasize Disagreement. If you say, "I don't agree with you" or "You're absolutely wrong," the other person will prepare to fight. It's more effective to give him credit for what he has said and then point out your position. Avoid dogmatic statements; use questions if they are appropriate.

Look for Areas of Agreement. There is usually some part of the other person's statement that you can accept, even though you may not agree with his or her main point. If you harp on the area of disagreement, you naturally promote the argument.

State the Other Person's Point Accurately and Fairly. In the very act of doing this you may gain a better understanding of it; you may even accept it partially. But state it accurately; don't just put words into the other person's mouth.

Back Up Your Own Position. Of course you must advance your position and back it up. But your reasoning should be sound and your facts accurate. Bring to bear as much evidence as possible to back up your point of view.

Avoiding an argument obviously takes more than a firm resolution to refuse to argue. It takes practice to apply these suggestions whenever an argument seems imminent, but the results are worthwhile. Chief among those results (on the assumption that you are correct) is recognition of your good judgment and tenacity in the face of opposition—two characteristics associated with people who deserve to get ahead.

Learn from the Mistakes of Others

It goes without saying that you ought to learn from your own mistakes. But a less trodden path toward recognition is the demonstrated ability to learn from others' errors.

Learning how someone else handled a blooper not only helps you anticipate and avoid committing a similar error yourself; it's good for your morale to verify the fact that no one is perfect.

LIBRARY
College of St. Francis
JOLIET, ILL.

101325

Since everyone pulls a boner at one time or another, you have the whole wide world to draw from. However, there are several kinds of people whose errors you may come into intimate contact with. Turn the knowledge you gain from their mistakes to your advantage.

Friends.   Whether or not the people you know socially do the same kind of work as you is not important. It's the general circumstances that led to their error that can be of value to you. Sarah Davis misjudged a prospect's motivations and lost a big order? It can be worth real money to you to discover precisely how she erred. Joe Dempster's office has been robbed? Get the details—and check your own office for the oversights that aided the burglars. Edna Harris goofed royally in preparing a budget proposal? Find out how, and draw a moral from it. Admittedly, not everybody is willing to discuss his or her mistakes. But, depending on the closeness of your relationship and your ability to draw the other person out tactfully, you can learn a great deal from your friends.

Fellow Workers.   The man next to you forgets to use his safety glasses and sustains an eye injury; the woman at the desk beside yours neglects to check over the letters your mutual secretary types for her and consequently hurts the feelings of an important customer; another of your firm's employees neglects to check out some facts and turns in an inaccurate report. Each of these co-workers' mistakes contains built-in lessons that are yours for the asking. Just keep your eyes and ears open.

Subordinates.   The people who work for you are bound to slip up now and then. Undo the damage whenever possible, of course, but don't stop there. Get to the root of the problem and find out why things went wrong. It will help you; it will help them; and properly examined, it will enable you to help other subordinates avoid similar mistakes in the future.

Your Boss.   Whether the person you report to is a supervisor, manager, or president, he too makes errors. After you have finished gloating, think his mistake through. What can you learn from it? This can be particularly valuable if you are working for the day when you will be considered for the job he now holds.

Your Competitors.   Whether it's a rival company or an individual, the mistakes made by your competitors can be of real dollars-and-cents value to you. If a competitor's promotion campaign has fizzled, for example, examine it with a view toward avoiding a repetition of his errors. If you hear that a competitive sales rep has alienated a mutual prospect by being too aggressive, take the hint and tone down your own presentation. You study your competitor's successes to see how you can profit from them. Do the same thing with his failures.

Famous People.   Because so much of a celebrity's life is open to all, his mistakes are frequently in the "public domain." You're a businessman? Publications like *Forbes, Fortune,* and *The Wall Street Journal* frequently run in-depth profiles of famous industrial figures, reporting their setbacks as well as their triumphs. You're a sales representative? You can find out a great deal about what *not* to do by reading the specialized books and articles by and about famous sales people. No matter what you do for a living, the most prominent and successful people in your field have almost certainly told their stories somewhere. Find them and learn! You'll be doing yourself a favor and, in the process, impressing your boss with your desire to improve your performance.

Pay Attention to the Little Things

In every organization there are men and women who enjoy reputations for personal performance that outshine all others. They are not necessarily smarter or more experienced or harder working than their colleagues. But in their day-to-day activities and behavior, they continually demonstrate certain traits of character that set them apart from the crowd and make them memorable. Here are six such characteristics. Try adapting them to your own situation.

The Wise Word.   When you speak, speak only about what you really know. Let your words carry weight because you don't speak them lightly.

The Kept Promise.   When you give a promise, move heaven and earth to live up to it. Let people be sure your word is your bond.

The Completed Job.   When you undertake anything, finish it. Build a reputation as a person who is thorough and sees things through.

The Extra Value.   Do more than is required just to get by. This is something that people really remember. It provides you with a sense of accomplishment too—and pays handsome dividends in warm personal relations.

Punctuality. Time is a limited asset. To waste another person's time by being unpunctual is to steal from him what he can never recover. Be on time.

Dependability. You will command respect in direct proportion to the number of people who have confidence that you will not let them down in any situation.

These are the traits that, in combination, spell integrity. If you make them synonymous with yourself you will find your reputation immeasurably enhanced. The recognition of others is, beyond argument, crucial to your personal success. But equally important is what you think of yourself, for it shines through everything you do. To make sure that you have good reason to think well of yourself, let us now turn our attention to the intriguing area of self-confidence.

4

Secrets of Self-Confidence

He was so ugly, tall, and ungainly that people nicknamed him "the gorilla." He had less than one year of schoolroom education. His father was a poor farmer; his mother, an illegitimate child; his wife, a shrew. He entered business—and went bankrupt. He ran for the United States Senate—and was defeated. He applied for an appointment to the United States Land Office—and was rejected. If ever a man seemed destined to total, unremitting failure, this man did. Acutely aware of his shortcomings, tormented by doubts as to his abilities, subject to periods of melancholia, on at least one occasion he seriously considered suicide.

Yet he overcame his doubts and, as president of the United States, led a divided nation through its ordeal by fire. As commander-in-chief of the Union Army, Abraham Lincoln attacked the problems of a civil war with surpassing skill and decisiveness. His death was mourned even by those who opposed him in life.

A young Hungarian, almost as tall as Lincoln, arrived in America at the age of seventeen. His reed-thin body supported a bulbous head with a small pointed chin and big nose. His English was marred by a thick foreign accent. Although he studied law and passed the bar, the twin handicaps of appearance and speech stood in the way of a successful practice. Afraid that he would be unable to support himself and regretting having left his homeland, in desperation he took a job as a reporter on a German-language newspaper in St. Louis. Reporters from other papers taunted him about his looks and speech. A stranger in an alien land, he toyed with the idea of returning to his native city of Budapest.

Yet, at thirty-one he was owner and publisher of the *St. Louis Post-Dispatch.* In the years that followed, Joseph Pulitzer bought the *New York World* and became one of the greatest, most influential publishers of all time.

In 1917 a salesman with the Fidelity Mutual Life Insurance Company was bemoaning his dismal failure. He was burdened by a terrible fear that made him freeze in the presence of prospects. So low had his morale sagged that be began to answer want ads for shipping clerks.

Yet thirty years later not only was he still selling insurance policies, but many of them were running into six figures. Frank Bettger, a confessed failure at twenty-eight, became one of America's top ten salespeople.

By all the rules, we should never have heard of these men. They had no right to succeed. Yet they did.

Why? How?

The answers to those questions include such predictable factors as hard work, self-discipline, a burning desire to succeed, and the conscious cultivation in these men of the skills they lacked. But there must have been some decisive force beneath their drive that ignited and kept aflame the will to succeed—a belief in themselves so unshakable that it could rise triumphantly above indifference, discouragement, and rejection. Somewhere along the line these men picked up the propelling energy and determination that comes from being sure of oneself.

These three—a president, a publisher, a sales representative—belonged to an elite segment of the population; the fairly small group that makes things happen. For it's a fact: Most people are unsure, insecure, scared of making up their own minds. They are controlled from without, not from within. For every Lincoln, Pulitzer, and Bettger, there are tens of thousands of others resigned to mediocrity or failure.

The sad fact of the matter is that they themselves have chosen mediocrity or failure. For self-confidence, like your vocabulary, is something you must build into yourself. No one—not even a king—is *born* with self-assurance.

If you are tired of being half sure, of indecision and self-doubt, if you truly want to think, act, feel and look self-confident, you can. It's entirely up to you.

Lack of Confidence

Why do so many people lack confidence? What specifically, makes them think that they are inferior to their fellows? In short, what forces shape the ninety-seven men out of a hundred who are unsure of themselves?

The confidence killers that follow are most frequently the culprits.

Before you learn the techniques for increasing your self-confidence, see how many of these counterproductive forces are currently interfering with your just appreciation of yourself.

Failure.   An idea you considered foolproof doesn't pan out. A decision you reached proves to be the wrong one. The results of weeks of hard work go down the drain. Everything you touch seems to turn to ashes. How long, you wonder, can anyone be expected to believe in himself under such circumstances?

The antidote: See failure for what it really is, an important learning experience and one major avenue to self-knowledge. Examined thoughtfully and viewed positively, failure can help you improve your performance by providing new insights into your personal weaknesses (perhaps a tendency to act rashly, a penchant for substituting wishful thinking for facing facts, the bad habit of starting projects with too little preparation).

An Ego-shaking Experience.   At one time or another, everyone has been exposed to an ego-rocking experience. A presentation goes badly. The boss chews you out. The biggest sale of your career is canceled. A promotion passes you by. From one bad experience you generalize that you are unworthy, unskilled, undeserving. Your confidence nosedives.

The antidote: Be rational. No scientist would dare draw a conclusion on the flimsy evidence of a few experiments. He would run hundreds, perhaps thousands of tests before he was satisfied that his conclusions were valid. The same applies to you. Flunk as a speaker? You'll have other chances to prove yourself. Boss been barking? Recall the compliments he's paid you in the past. That sale? Remember the times *you* beat the competition. Promotion fall through? Look where you are today, compared to where you were five years ago. In other words, don't rate yourself solely on temporary setbacks. Weigh all the evidence.

Worry.   Given a new assignment, you wonder if you're smart enough, capable enough, or experienced enough to carry it off. After all, a thousand different things may go wrong. Suppose you can't dig up the necessary data? What if you underestimated the number of people needed for the project? When can you possibly find the time to squeeze this job into your heavy schedule? You can see yourself falling flat on your face and hear your boss raking you over the coals right now.

The antidote: Worry is one of the great energy sappers, and whether you face a strenuous job or an imminent deadline, you'll need all the stamina you can muster. So stay calm. Don't jump to conclusions about the outcome. To help you maintain your perspective, consider this Worry Table:

What Most People Worry About

Things that don't come to pass	40%
Things that can't be changed by all the worry in the world	35%
Things that turn out better than expected	15%
Petty, useless worries	8%
Legitimate worries	2%

Since the odds are fifty to one against your worry being a legitimate cause for concern, why take such a long shot seriously?

False Assumptions. "That V.P. has never liked me." "When you're born on the wrong side of the tracks, you stay there." "Nobody's interested in my opinion." "Without connections, you're dead." Such formulaic thinking paralyzes initiative and destroys self-confidence in a most comforting way, for it takes matters out of your hands. "They" are against you, and that's all there is to it.

The antidote: Recognize such assumptions for the poor excuses that they are and get on to the business at hand. Few of us are the victims of a concerted plot. Our bosses do *not* lie awake at night dreaming up ways to frustrate our plans, our work, the realization of our goals. Our co-workers are *not* continually scheming to undo our accomplishments. In other words, in 999 out of every 1,000 cases, *we* are the architects of our destiny, the moving force behind what happens to us, the final cause of how we act and what we do. Think of all the successful people who have risen above their backgrounds, their limitations, their handicaps.

Lack of Formal Education. Because you never completed college, or high school, or elementary school, you feel that you couldn't possibly compete with people who have. You are hopelessly outdistanced. Why, then, should you have faith in your own abilities? This kind of self-effacement stems from the belief that a diploma is an all-powerful open sesame to success. Do you believe that the lack of a formal education is an insuperable barrier to success?

The antidote: First, realize that "educated" is not a label that is won by attending a university for four years. Rather, it reflects an attitude. If you have an open, inquiring mind and want to learn, you possess the most important requisites for being "educated." Second, pursue a course of home study in whatever fields interest you most. Get to know your local library. Keep abreast of news in your particular field by reading pertinent trade and technical journals.

Pessimistic Friends. To a large extent, our personalities are shaped by the people with whom we associate, on the job and off. At one time or another, for example, everyone has caught himself using an expression or gesture learned from a friend. The same holds true of beliefs and attitudes. Talk long enough to a pessimist, the kind of person who sees a beautiful sunrise as the beginning of another rotten day, and you will soon view the world through the same prism of hopelessness. A woman whose friends continually complain about their health, their jobs, their bad breaks, the way people treat them, and the generally hopeless state of the universe is bound to form a "what's-the-use?" attitude toward everything. People are no damn good—and that includes her. Right?

The antidote: Avoid inveterate crepehangers like the plague! Cultivate the friendship of optimists. They're not hard to spot. There's bounce in their walk, bubble in their talk, and they know how to smile. It's a tonic to be near them.

Laziness. It's easier to sit still than to move, to keep quiet than to talk, to dream than to act. But confidence is largely based on action. If you don't *do* anything, you'll never know what you're capable of. And how can you be confident about an unknown quantity? People who are lazy seldom admit it. Instead, they "haven't the time," "don't feel up to it right now," "can't be bothered."

The antidote: Analyze the reasons for your inertia. Are they valid? If they aren't, face up to it and delay no longer. Take the first step toward your goal today—even if it's only drawing up a list of things to do or dialing the phone. The important thing is to get the ball rolling.

Illness. It is impossible to do your best when you're not feeling well because part of your body's resources are either out of commission or attending to the business of combating illness. And since self-confidence depends partially on the knowledge that you are working at peak performance, sickness is bound to undermine it.

The antidote: See a doctor if that below-par feeling persists; a complete physical every year if you are over forty is strongly recommended; and a dental checkup should be a semiannual affair. Get adequate rest, some exercise, and fresh air; watch your weight and eat sensibly.

Lack of Job Knowledge. There are few confidence killers as deadly as lack of job knowledge. The person who knows, and knows that he knows, has no hesitations or fears when confronted by a situation he is equipped to meet, for "familiarity breeds attempt." The person faced by a task beyond his knowledge, however, is foredoomed to failure and, therefore, diminished self-confidence. Are there any serious gaps in your knowledge of your own job?

The antidote: If possible, take refresher courses or attend seminars in your area of expertise. Acquire the habit of holding informal bull sessions with people in your field. Ask questions of your superiors. Don't hesitate to learn from subordinates. Practice the techniques of your job whenever possible.

Excessive Humility. This frequently stems from the belief that the only alternative is overweening pride. Not so. There is a middle ground: self-confidence, which is no more nor less than the proper appreciation of your worth as a human being. By constantly throwing your shortcomings into high relief, excessive humility gives you and others a distorted picture of your overall abilities.

The antidote: Will Rogers said it: "Everyone is ignorant, only on different subjects." Accept the fact that everyone has limitations, including you. But don't dwell on your shortcomings. Instead, take a look at your plus side. If necessary, draw up a list of your personal assets and accomplishments and study it.

Although ridding yourself of the confidence killers in your life is an excellent beginning, it is not enough. That would be like pumping all the stale air out of a room and neglecting to replace it with clean, fresh air. Nothing can flourish in a vacuum. It is now up to you to create the positive environment in which self-confidence thrives.

Know Your Stuff

A computer operator isn't the least bit intimidated by the black boxes, flashing lights, video screens, and clattering printers that are incomprehensible to you and me. Hundreds of feet above the ground, a high-wire performer nonchalantly goes about a job that leaves the rest of us breathless. A surgeon enters an operating room and approaches a nervous patient with a supreme confidence no layman can fathom. Why?

Because each of these specialists knows his or her job: *what* to do, *how* it's done, *why* it's done.

You, too, must know your stuff. Know it inside out. Saturate yourself in it. There's nothing that will put the spring of self-assurance into your walk and into your performance like being sure that you definitely know what you are doing.

Determine Your Strengths and Weaknesses

No doctor would prescribe medicine or treatment for a person he knew nothing about. First, he would ask questions: What kind of pain is the patient suffering from? Where is it located? Has he ever experienced the pain before? When? How often? And so on. Only after he has learned as much as possible from the patient would he begin his physical examination.

In order to increase your self-confidence, you must do the same thing—with one important difference. You must be your own doctor.

Since no two people are identical, you must first discover precisely what your own strong and weak points are. Only then can you take the proper corrective measures—for you.

So the first order of business is to draw a "confidence profile" of yourself. This will identify your current strengths and weaknesses and give you some idea of where you must work harder.

Since no one but you can draw such a profile, you will have to be brutally frank with yourself and face up to your shortcomings. Most of us have little trouble pinpointing those areas in which we are strong; our weaknesses sometimes prove more elusive. To get you started, here are some questions to answer.

Do you enter easily into conversation with strangers?
Do you dread the idea of speaking before a group of people?
Do you worry excessively over what others think of you?
Do you accept constructive criticism graciously?
Do you ever point out errors to your superiors?
Do you consider yourself uninteresting?
Do you have the courage to speak your mind against opposition?

Do you ever take decisive action on your job without consulting your superior?

Under what circumstances do you feel most ill at ease?

We seldom stop to analyze our own weaknesses, and it can be a painful exercise to do so. But since remedial action depends largely on facing the facts, it is a necessary step toward the bolstering of self-confidence. Take your time and take stock of your strengths and weaknesses.

Follow a Self-Development Plan

Every top athlete does it. Why shouldn't you? A boxer whose timing is off will spend hours in the gym crouched before a sandbag, practicing his one-two punch until he develops machine-gun rapidity. A basketball star who performs poorly from the foul line will shoot practice baskets for hours. A baseball slugger whose nemesis is an outside pitch will have a pitcher from his own team throw outside balls to him throughout spring training.

However, no champion is content *only* with improving his weaknesses. He also spends grueling hours sharpening his strengths. Thus, a boxer with trigger reflexes will continue to shadow box until he has his reflexes up to *hair*-trigger standards. The basketball player whose forte is the lay-up shot continually practices his strongest point. The batter whose bunting ability wins games seeks constantly to perfect this skill.

The same applies to you. In order to increase your self-confidence, you must strengthen your weaknesses as well as build on your strengths.

This means that, having identified your weaknesses, you must consciously and consistently force yourself to overcome them. The best way is to take one at a time and concentrate on eliminating it from your character. If, for instance, you have discovered that you lack the courage to speak your mind against opposition, then for a week . . . or two . . . or three . . . or however long it may take, concentrate on that one weakness, forcing yourself, regardless of how distasteful you may find it, to stand up to opposing points of view.

And when you have finally conquered that weakness—and you will— then you go on to your second weakness, and your third, and so on. Once you have strengthened your weaknesses, you can turn your attention to building on your strengths.

Most people already do this unconsciously. A woman whose complexion is her outstanding feature will lavish hours on cleansing her skin, moisturizing it and experimenting with assorted colorings and shadings— all to enhance its natural beauty. A man who is an expert dancer will continually seek to improve his ability by learning new steps.

Most successful careers are founded on this unconscious tendency to build on strengths. A person with a flair for mathematics is naturally attracted to those fields requiring that special ability: finance, accountancy, bookkeeping. A man who enjoys literature gravitates toward teaching, writing, publishing. An extrovert might seek his fortune in selling, acting, politics, public relations.

What you must do is consciously harness your natural bent in order to build on your strengths. This will be far easier than strengthening your weaknesses, for your strengths are assets that you already possess. It's largely a matter of identifying them. Once you have them firmly in mind, treat them as you did your weaknesses. Devote a week, or two , or three to building each of them up. If, for example, you find that you perform well in front of others, seek out opportunities to address groups of people, either formally or informally, until you have honed that particular strength into a formidable advantage.

Develop Enthusiasm

The late Frederick Williamson, president of the New York Central Railway, was once asked what he thought was the secret of success in business. This is what he answered: "The longer I live, the more certain I am that enthusiasm is the little-recognized secret of success. The difference in actual skill and ability and intelligence between those who succeed and those who fail is usually neither wide nor striking. But if two men are nearly equally matched, the man who is enthusiastic will find the scales tipped in his favor. And a man of second-rate ability *with enthusiasm* will often outstrip one of first-rate ability *without enthusiasm.* Enthusiasm means believing in your work and loving it, be it digging a ditch or directing a great company. To an enthusiastic man, his work is always part play, no matter how hard or demanding it is. If a man is in this frame of mind, he is bound for the stars and success."

Here are some ways to develop chronic enthusiasm.

• Learn all you can about your job and how it fits into the big picture. Many people feel like mere cogs in a giant machine simply because they do not understand the ramifications of their work—what it does for others, how it is beneficial to the economy and to society. But appreciate how much you are really contributing and you cannot help but feel enthusiastic (see "Know Your Job." p. 20).

• Think of all the people who depend on you—on the job and off. It will perk you up like magic.

• Improve your perspective by comparing where you are today with where you were five or ten years ago. The odds are that you are earning more (in real dollars), have more free time, and are a little closer to the realization of your life's goals.

• Associate with enthusiastic people. Just as it is practically impossible to be an optimist among pessimists, so it is impossible to be enthusiastic amidst people who drag their feet and minds around the dull routine of daily duties. But mix with men and women who are excited about their work, interested in the world in all its diversity and in the future and some of their enthusiasm is bound to rub off.

Master Fear

According to an old Arabic story, Pestilence met a caravan on the road to Baghdad.

"Why are you making such great haste to Baghdad?" asked the leader of the caravan.

"To take five thousand lives," Pestilence replied.

On the way back from the city Pestilence and the caravan met again.

"You lied!" the leader cried angrily. "You took not five thousand lives, but fifty thousand!"

"No," said Pestilence. "I took five thousand only and not one more. It was Fear who killed the rest."

Fear is still the greatest killer in the world. It murders ambition, daring, achievement—and confidence.

The factory worker who trembles every time her supervisor inspects her work, the office worker who shivers in his shoes whenever the boss summons him, the junior executive who doubts her ability to assume more responsibility, the middle manager who fancies that he feels the hot breath of some ambitious young tiger on his neck—all these men and women are stabbing themselves in the back with the treacherous knife of fear.

Some fears, of course, like that of falling, exist to protect life. They are purposeful and cannot be altered by an exercise of will. But nameless, irrational, paralyzing fear maims the mind and poisons life. That kind of fear lacks roots in fact or reason; but it feeds on the heart of unthinking emotion.

Fear Is the Natural Reaction to Every Unknown Situation.

Read that sentence over and over until you completely comprehend its meaning, for it is a sentence that can remove a great part of the negative power of fear.

Since fear is the natural reaction to every unknown situation, it follows that it may be successfully combatted with knowledge. If you are afraid of a dark room, you switch on the light and your fears are dissolved. Once you grow acquainted with a stranger, you no longer fear him. When we understand, we do not fear.

The best way to throw the light of understanding on a fear is to analyze it. The first thing to do is to admit your fear; this is frequently the most difficult part. All of us rationalize to some extent, and it is hard to admit the truth even to ourselves. But unacknowledged fears are the ones that do the most harm. We vaguely feel their presence but hate to concede their existence. Admit freely that your fear exists, however, and half the battle is won. Then ask yourself *why* you have this fear. If your heart skips a beat when the boss asks you into his office, pause for a moment and examine the reasons for your fear. Are you afraid of some criticism? Why? What have you done wrong? Do you fear being fired? Why? Have you been inefficient, lazy, stupid, dishonest, unethical? No? Then there is nothing to fear.

It is often helpful to write your fear down on paper, where you can confront it openly and see, once and for all, what it is that has been nagging at you. There is a world of difference between an undefined fear of impending doom and reading the sentence, "I'm afraid that my request for a transfer is going to be turned down." In the first case, the vagueness of the fear multiplies its power over you; in the second, you can see that even if your worst fear materializes, the consequences are far from tragic.

Analyze your fear and you will be well on the way to mastering it.

Conquer the Physical Expressions of Fear

In 1884 the great American psychologist, William James, published an article that caused a sensation in scientific circles. Its title: "What is an Emotion?" In it James advanced a startling new theory. He said that although people had always assumed that first they perceived an emotion-provoking situation, then had an emotional experience, and finally behaved emotionally, he was convinced that the sequence of events was incorrect.

People had always believed, for example, that (a) you meet a bear; (b) you are frightened; and (c) you run away. But James maintained that this was wrong. The correct sequence, he suggested, is: (a) you meet a bear; (b) you run away; and (c) you are frightened.

In other words, an emotional experience is the perception of bodily changes. *You don't run away because you are afraid; you are afraid because you run away!*

To support his theory James claimed that unless you assumed the posture typical to an emotion, you could not experience that emotion. That is, if a situation calls for grief and instead of slumping you hold your head high and stick out your chest, you will experience far less grief. On the other hand, if you assume the posture typical of a certain emotion, you will be more readily subject to that emotion. (Actors use this approach in the simulation of emotions with good results.)

James's theory, widely accepted in some circles, has enormous possibilities for anyone seeking to master fear. Consider the ways in which fear manifests itself; quickened pulse, shortness of breath, inner trembling, hot and cold sensations. All these expressions of fear are the direct result of tensions within your body. Get rid of those tensions and you will rid yourself of the expressions of fear. Rid yourself of the expressions of fear and you will rid yourself of the fear itself!

This is how to do it: Next time you find yourself getting scared, drop your lower jaw, take a big breath, yawn, and release your breath with a sigh. Do this several times until your entire body feels relaxed.

Another remedy is to do what you fear to do and the knowledge and experience gained will in themselves allay anxiety. Are you afraid to meet people? Then do it again and again so that you may realize how groundless your fears are. Are you afraid to speak to an audience? If you do it only once or twice, you may never quite conquer your fear. But stand up in public at every available opportunity and you will steadily whittle away at your fear. Admittedly, it is very difficult to force yourself to do something against which every fiber of your being rebels. But the second time is easier than the first, and the third easier than the second, and the tenth easier than the ninth. Psychologists call this process desensitization.

Do what you fear to do, and in ninety-eight cases out of a hundred you will conquer the anxiety.

Act Confident

Dash into a burning building, sweep a crying child into your arms, run out—and you're a hero. Study the greatest thoughts of the greatest men—and you're a scholar. "A man is what he does."

What has this to do with increasing your self-confidence? Just this: If you look, sound, and feel confident—in short, if you *act* confident—you will *be* confident.

Your Appearance. Study the person whom you most admire for his self-confidence. Always well dressed, isn't he? It's more than mere chance. There is a strong connection between the two. Don't misunderstand. The well-dressed man is not always dressed to the teeth. He is always dressed appropriately: in business clothes at the office; in clean, comfortable work clothes at his machine; in knockabout slacks when working on his lawn or in his home workshop. If self-confidence is based largely on knowledge (and it is), then knowing that you look your best can only boost it.

Your Attitude. Every year police around the world arrest men and women who make their dishonest livings by selling to gullible customers diamonds made of glass, "lost treasure" maps, and nonexistent uranium mines. Invariably, the victims of a con man sheepishly admit that they fell for the scheme because "he sounded so sure of himself." Speak to any of these criminals and you are immediately struck by the aura of self-confidence that seems to surround him. Mainly, you notice the way he speaks. His vocabulary is good, often impressive; his grammar, impeccable; his pronunciation, excellent. And because he *sounds* confident, you tend to take him at face value. That is why police bunco squads are always kept busy. Don't turn criminal, of course, but take a tip from the con man: Sound confident.

Your Self-Image.   A final barrier that can stand between a person and the achievement of complete self-confidence is the feeling of inferiority. The important thing here is to bear in mind that *everybody* has such feelings. One man may suffer untold pain because he is short, a second because he is unattractive, a third because he is physically weak, a fourth because he stutters. The reasons for inferiority feelings are as varied as human nature. The only difference between a confident person and an unconfident one rests on the former's ability to make his sense of inferiority work for him.

Psychologists have discovered that people react to their feelings of inferiority in a variety of ways. Four of the most important are *aggression, rationalization, regression,* and *overcompensation.* For example, take a young man who is thin and weak and who feels inferior to all the young men with fine physiques he sees about him. Such a young man might react to his feelings of unworthiness by buying a gun and becoming a killer. By thus "proving" how tough he is, he makes up for his feelings of inadequacy. He has reacted to his sense of inferiority with aggression.

The same young man might say to himself, "My poor physical development isn't my fault. Such things are hereditary. My parents gave me this sorry body. I'm stuck with it and that's that." This explanation absolves him of responsibility and assuages his pride. He has reacted to his inferiority with rationalization.

Or the young man might seek a way out of his dilemma by taking advantage of his frail condition. He might turn hypochondriac, a sickly boy who must be taken care of by his mother. If he can once again establish the mother-baby relationship, he can remove himself from invidious comparisons with other young men his age. He tries to do this by turning back the clock, in terms of emotion, to the time when mama took care of him. He has reacted with regression.

Finally, the young man might decide to develop his muscles through a program of exercise. He might lift weights, box, wrestle, swim, and run until his body ripples with muscles. He might do this for years, until his physique surpasses that of everyone else, until he looks like a god. He has reacted with overcompensation.

At least one man did precisely that. His name was Angelo Siciliano, better known as Charles Atlas, "the world's most perfectly developed man." Conceivably, Mr. Siciliano could have turned into a hoodlum, a whiner, or a hypochondriac. Instead, he chose a healthy answer to his inferiority complex and licked it in spades.

Winston Churchill stuttered terribly as a boy; he became one of our century's foremost orators.

O.J. Simpson had to wear braces on his legs as a boy; as a result of exercise and pure grit, he became what many consider to be the best running back in football history.

Arthur Murray was a tall, gangling youth, sadly lacking in the social graces; today his name is still synonymous with grace and dancing ability.

These men made their feelings of inferiority work for them. So can you.

Of course, it is sometimes impossible to overcompensate. A short man cannot turn into a giant through years of discipline or determination. A blind woman, no matter how much she may work at it, cannot develop hawklike eyesight. But every person, regardless of his or her short-comings, can cultivate a substitute quality.

So Alexander Pope, four and one-half feet tall, deformed and hump-backed, so weak that he could not rise from bed unaided, wrote some of the most polished verse of the eighteenth century.

Isaac Newton, among science's most original thinkers, was severely beaten by a bully when he was a boy. Until then he had been an ordinary student. Deciding that he would never excel with his fists, he concentrated on developing his brain.

Voltaire, the French philosopher, was an extraordinarily ugly man who found the cultivation of a keen wit more than an adequate substitute for good looks. Indeed, it was said that after one spoke with him for ten minutes, his face seemed to turn positively handsome.

There are two ways, then, to handle an inferiority complex. You may improve the quality you most lack, as did Angelo Siciliano. Or you may find one or more substitute qualities to develop, as Alexander Pope and Sir Isaac Newton did. The important thing is to recognize that you need not accept your current inadequacies as ineradicable. They can be modified or eliminated.

5

Winning Habits:
How to Cultivate Them

One secret of success is, "Choose rich parents." Another is, "Buy low; sell high." Those of us who missed out on the first, and still haven't gotten the hang of the second, have to seek out other avenues.

One suggestion: identify and cultivate the habits that characterize winners. But what, exactly, are they? They consist of a number of things with only one common factor: They are invariably part of the makeup of every successful person, regardless of his or her industry or specialty. Acquire these habits yourself, make them part and parcel of your personal equipment, and you should be well on your way to being a winner yourself.

The Habit of Learning

Winners have learned how to learn. They understand that this crucial skill has become the recognized passport to success in our time, for ours is an age of specialists and experts.

This endless demand for knowledge really means an endless demand for people who continue to learn. There is not a field you can name that has not changed drastically within the last decade and that will not continue to do so. Are you an executive? Almost daily new theories are born on such subjects as business planning, cost analysis and control, marketing strategies, and sales forecasting. Are you a technician? Scores of books and hundreds of articles on your specialty roll off the presses annually. Are you in sales? There have been startling advances in the psychology of persuasion.

In order to grow, succeed, and advance, you must keep up with the new discoveries, ideas, and techniques in your own special field and the wide, wide world beyond it. There is only one way to keep pace with the enormous changes going on all around you. It is to learn as much as you can about them—their whys, wheres, whens, whos, and hows. And be-

44

cause new knowledge is accumulating faster than ever before, it is necessary to master it as efficiently as possible. In other words, *you must learn
how to learn.*

The following rules will help you:

Intend to Learn. Without batting an eyelash, some otherwise ordinary
people can reel off the fluctuations in price , and the histories, of a whole
series of common stocks for the last decade. You yourself are probably
well versed in at least one particular field—automobiles, carpentry, skin
diving, current best sellers, World War II.

In each case the particular reason for a special interest may vary (the
influence of a favorite teacher, the desire for social approval, the possibility of monetary reward, etc.), but the basic reason remains the same:
There is a fundamental intention to learn the subject. Psychologists call
this bending of one's energies toward a given end *mental set,* and it
affects learning as well as other activities. The things we intend to learn
are much more apt to be mastered than other things that we observe,
hear, or read.

The first step toward learning anything, then, is to intend to learn. One
of the best ways to strengthen this intention is to sell yourself on the
benefits of learning the material in question. Will it help you solve a
tough problem, make more money, win prestige? Mentally list the
rewards you will derive from your new knowledge. If you truly want
them, you will learn.

Concentrate on Accuracy. A mistake once learned is repeated until it
is firmly entrenched and difficult to eliminate. To learn something incorrectly, unlearn it, then relearn it correctly, is obviously triple work.
You can reduce your learning work load by two-thirds, therefore, if you
determine to get things right the first time. Some tips:

• Forget about speed. Trying to assimilate information quickly more
often defeats than serves its purpose. Slower, more accurate learning is
actually faster in the long run.
• Study only when you are in condition. There is a law of diminishing
returns in learning. If boredom or fatigue sets in, attention—and hence,
learning—nosedives.
• Take frequent breaks. Experiments have confirmed the efficiency of
distributing learning over a period of time. By interrupting your learning

from time to time, you literally give the information you have acquired an opportunity to sink in. One caution: Do not use the intervals between study sessions to study related material; it sets up interference.

Seek to Understand.   Study the following two lines.

A. Geoffrey Chaucer was the father of the English language.

B. Kroylans Vintlah nup mab hortch ik mil kirbixy moognatz.

Undoubtedly, you had no difficulty absorbing the information contained in sentence A. Sentence B, however, is another story. Although it contains the same number of characters as A, it is far more difficult to remember, for it has no meaning.

There are two ways to learn: by rote and by understanding. Some things, like telephone numbers, must be learned by rote. Information learned by understanding, however, is retained much longer than information that is merely memorized.

To prove it to yourself, take out a pencil and a sheet of paper. Look at sentence A above for about five seconds. Then cover it with your hand and try to reproduce the information it contains. Now study line B for the same length of time and try to reproduce it. Almost impossible, isn't it?

If you were asked to duplicate these two lines tomorrow, next week, or next month, you would find that while you might not get sentence A letter-perfect, you would still remember the gist of it. With the passage of time and no further practice, however, line B would become hopelessly garbled in your mind.

Never be satisfied with only a hazy idea of what you are studying. This cannot be sufficiently emphasized. Learning a thing means understanding it. You cannot absorb and remember what you never knew in the first place. So if you are not able to follow an idea, go back to where you lost the trail and tackle it again, or if you are listening to someone, ask the speaker to clarify his explanation. Don't consider it learned until you really understand it.

Look for General Principles.   In a famous experiment, a group of college students was divided into two teams. One team memorized the solutions to a series of match tricks, while the other memorized the principles *behind* the solutions. A month later the two teams were tested on what they had learned. The majority of those who memorized without understanding the principles exhibited marked and rapid forgetting. On the other hand, most of those who learned the principles demonstrated almost perfect retention.

From your own experience, you know that mastery of a general principle is one of the basic keys to learning. When you first studied arithmetic, for example, you were taught how to multiply such numbers as 9×6, 27×18, and 249×131. However, you were not taught how to multiply every possible number by every other possible number or you would still be working on it. After a certain amount of drilling on the *principles* of multiplication, you understood the general idea behind it. Today you would have no trouble multiplying $564{,}783 \times 585{,}769$, not because you had ever multiplied those two particular numbers before but because you learned the principles of multiplying any number by any other number.

There are few better short cuts to efficient learning than the assimilation of principles. Mastery of a general principle places less of a burden on your memory than would the memorization of all the specific facts that comprise it. It prepares you for understanding future information that is based on it. Most importantly, it helps you to organize future facts and ideas by providing large "mental compartments" for them.

Whenever possible, therefore, try to spot basic principles in what you are studying. They are far more important than the specific examples used to illustrate or back them up.

Harness the Laws of Memory. Almost everyone has experienced the frustration and embarrassment of having allowed some piece of urgent business to go unattended simply because he forgot about it. In retrospect it seems impossible that you can blank out on performing a specific task, but during the press of the workday, there it goes—into oblivion.

You can improve your memory for chores and everything else by harnessing these four laws on your behalf.

The Law of Association. If two or more things are experienced or heard together frequently enough, the presence of one elicits the recall of the other. Just as we learn by association, so we remember by it too. We recall the things that are easier to remember and then make the transfer to the more difficult. Therefore, the things to be remembered and used together should be learned together.

The Law of Succession. If two or more things are frequently experienced in immediate succession, the presence of the first tends to trigger recall of the other. For example, sometimes it is difficult to remember offhand what letter of the alphabet comes before another, but recite the letters in sequence and there you are! The great advantage to learning in succession is that when you remember one item in a list, you recall the next, then the next, and so forth.

The Law of Similarity. If two things are similar, the thought of one causes the recall of the other.

The Law of Contrast. If you've ever daydreamed about a sunny beach while waiting for a bus in a snowstorm, then you know that extremes or opposites serve as reminders of each other. When you think of the tallest person you've ever seen, you may also think of the shortest. The use of contrast improves the vividness of the impression and the ability to recall.

Build on What You Already Know. Shortly after its founding, the United Nations faced a critical situation. No one could be found to translate an important document into Albanian. A French translator offered to learn the language and translate the document in just four days. To the astonishment of UN officials he was able to do precisely what he had promised—without error, as it turned out—within the specified period. How did he do it? He had already learned twenty languages and had acquired know-how in the area of mastering foreign tongues.

You yourself probably know someone who can absorb new information on a particular subject with astounding ease. Why? One reason is that that person already possesses an extensive knowledge of the subject. In effect, his or her mind is filled with hooks on which to hang new facts and ideas.

When you come across a new fact or idea, therefore, make a conscious effort to relate it to information with which you are already familiar. The relationship may be strictly logical, such as when a new method of taking inventory is learned by comparing and contrasting it with a method already known. Or the relationship may be contrived, as when an important date is linked in the mind with a number that has a personal importance to you. For example, you want to remember the year 1876. If you were born in 1946, you might remember to subtract 70 from your year of birth. The important thing is to find the hooks that already exist in your mind and hang new information from them.

Overlearn. You've never forgotten your own name, have you? If you analyzed the reason, you would find that because you had pronounced, signed, and responded to it so often in the course of your life, it had become indelibly engraved on your mind. You have overlearned it. *Everything* that you can recall without effort has been overlearned through frequent use.

In the language of psychology, *overlearning* does not mean "learning too much." Rather, it means "reviewing something that has already been learned sufficiently for one perfect recitation." Experiments consistently prove that there is a precise and favorable correlation between the extent of overlearning and the ability to remember material for a long period of time.

The rule, therefore, is simple and straightforward. After you have learned any given material up to the point of being able to repeat it smoothly, continue to drill yourself in it just as if you had not yet learned it.

The Habit of Thinking

Winners know that regardless of their specific responsibilities, their ability to think—precisely, thoroughly, originally—represents the most valuable contribution they can make to their companies. There are undoubtedly other men and women who can do what they do, perhaps not quite so well, but well enough to get the job done. But no one can duplicate another person's thought processes. So anything you can do to improve your thinking ability is additional success insurance.

Be Precise. As noted earlier, the overwhelming majority of people think in words. But if the words you use are too general, imprecise, or altogether wrong, your thinking will necessarily be sloppy. Suppose you say to yourself, "I can't depend on secretaries." That's a sweeping statement and may not actually be what you mean. You may really be thinking of one particular secretary and one particular instance of his or her undependability. But in your haste or because of a lack of inner discipline you generalized. The result: impaired thinking. To think effectively, you must use precise words.

Be Flexible. Just as bad as generalizing is rigidity. Beware of becoming too orderly in your thought processes. In order to think originally, you must be willing to allow your mind to wander, to strike out on its own, to go off onto tangents, to play with various possibilities.

Talk It Over. Find someone with whom you can exchange views. In effect, you will be talking out loud, and the opportunity to hear your thoughts sometimes provides new insights. The mere presence of another person tends to make you take a broader look at your approach.

Take Your Time. Nobody ever had a great idea in a hurry. Creative thinking is hard, demanding work. Ideas have to be critically assessed, reconsidered, modified, simplified, and tested. It's only human to over-rate our own ideas, especially when we are keyed up over a problem. Time permitting, sleep on it, and see if it still looks like a winner in the morning.

The Habit of Looking for Shortcuts

Winners get things done. They have an uncanny way of tackling a chore and disposing of it quickly and efficiently. Often, they manage to do this by identifying and using a variety of shortcuts.

This doesn't mean evading a job that needs to be done. It means working intelligently and making the most of all the resources at your disposal. No one can accuse you of shirking your duty if you are smart enough to know how to do it more easily, more quickly, and with less effort.

See the Opportunity in the Assignment. A tough assignment isn't a form of punishment. It is more like a compliment. If you are given a difficult job to do, it really means that your boss considers you ready for it. He has faith in your ability and is handing you—on a silver platter, at that—the opportunity to prove yourself. If you come through, you are bound to increase your chances for advancement and reward. Once you learn to view every new task in this light, you will have come a long way toward conquering the feeling of working under pressure that often prevents people from doing their very best. Free of worry, you can bend your energies to the task at hand.

Organize the Assignment. Just what are the duties thrust upon your shoulders? What are you supposed to accomplish? Surprisingly, few people ever take the time to think through a new job properly. Mistaking activity for accomplishment, they rush off in a dozen different directions at once, overexert themselves, and in reality get little done. If they would take twenty or thirty minutes to analyze the job before plunging in, they could save themselves a lot of needless wear and tear.

To organize the assignment, study it until you can see it as a series of parts, each with a beginning and an ending of its own. Each part in itself is not too frightening. In combination, the parts will eventually add up to a whole.

Pick Others' Brains.   The job you've been handed may be new and unfamiliar to you, but almost surely it's routine to somebody else. Very well, seek that person out and ask him for advice. From his experience he can doubtless help you find fresh ideas, new solutions, and additional sources of information.

The Habit of Hoarding Ideas

Winners never seem to be at a loss for good ideas. Their secret: They hoard them! Like those comedians who can fire a gag on any given subject at a moment's notice, they constantly gather useful ideas. How do they do it? One of the most effective systems is very simple.

You should already be in the habit of reading, listening, and absorbing material relevant to your needs or interests. In particular, follow the trade publications in the fields that interest you. They're gold mines of information.

When you note interesting items, cut them out, add your own notes right then and there, and staple them to a uniform-size sheet of paper. Write an identifying phrase in the upper right-hand corner. It will make it far easier to find the idea when needed. Then file the material in an appropriate place where you can locate it readily. Letter-size folders with paste-on labels are excellent for this purpose. These files can prove one of your best investments, for pertinent information on a wide variety of subjects is readily accessible.

The Habit of Establishing Subgoals

No matter how awesome a project may appear initially, it can always be broken down into a series of manageable steps.

Suppose, for example, that the boss asks you to submit a report analyzing production problems for the past ten years. Why not set each year's analysis as a subgoal? If you're studying a technical manual on the operation of a new piece of machinery, mastering each section could be set as a subgoal.

The point is that action breeds action, success breeds success. As you achieve each smaller goal, you will find your determination—and ability—to achieve the big goal gaining momentum.

To keep up the acceleration, use these techniques:

Dispose of the Simple Parts First.   If you were asked to pick a bushel of apples, what procedures would you follow? You would head for the orchard and first gather up the apples that had already fallen from the trees. Next, you would scan the lower branches for apples within easy reach. Only after you had taken full advantage of nature's help would you start climbing trees for out-of-reach apples. The same principle applies to every job you undertake: Get the obvious and routine out of the way first.

This approach offers two important psychological advantages. First, it provides a "warming-up" period. Boxers do it. Pitchers do it. Football teams do it. Why shouldn't you? By easing yourself into the work at hand, you get the mental and physical kinks out of your system. You establish a rhythm of accomplishment. And you gradually divest yourself of extraneous thoughts; you begin to concentrate on what you are doing to the exclusion of everything else.

Second, it bolsters your self-confidence. Once you see that you have some work accomplished, no matter how negligible it may be, you automatically create the impetus within yourself to drive further on. You begin to think, "Hey, I'm getting there!" And so you are.

No matter what the job or project, a few of its ingredients are bound to be familiar or akin to something you have handled before. Dispose of them first. Must you make an important decision? Chances are you already know some of the factors that must be weighed. Write them down immediately. Do you have to assemble a specialized report? You are undoubtedly acquainted with at least a few of the sources of information you can draw upon. Get to them.

The important thing is to get the ball rolling. It's the first, absolutely necessary, prelude to productivity.

Tackle the Most Difficult Parts Later.   You've warmed up. You're fresh, alert, in the swing of things. Now you're ready to tackle the toughest part of your job. Concentrate and work at it with all your might. Keep in mind that this is the most difficult part, and once it's done, the worst will be over for good. The rest will be relatively easy sledding.

Put Yourself on a Schedule.   By promising yourself that you will reach certain goals at specific points of time, you establish a positive frame of mind that actually makes those goals easier to reach. In drawing up your schedule, however, be sure to allow for profits and losses. Since the best-laid plans can go astray, be flexible enough to bounce back. If you find yourself ahead of schedule, reinvest the time gained in a little chore you thought you wouldn't get around to until tomorrow. If your schedule is unpredictably upset, reschedule as necessary.

The Habit of 20/20 Listening

Winners listen because they realize that most people have *something* worthwhile to say.

There are two basic techniques used by professional listeners such as newspaperpeople, psychoanalysts, and vocational counselors that can help you become a 20/20 listener. They are nondirective and directive listening. To the pro, these two techniques represent two ends of the same spectrum. What makes the difference is how extensively the listener gets into the act, whether he is a sponge or a cross-examiner.

For everyday use, you should know both techniques. Start with non-directive listening, allowing the speaker to run the show, quietly absorbing everything he or she says. As you begin to discern what's worth hearing, move into control. Eventually, you will arrive at the directive end of the scale. At this point, you run the conversation, choosing the things you want to hear more about.

Here are the five steps in the process. By following them and learning to apply them habitually, you can make your listening a far more profitable activity than it probably is now.

• Be receptive. A little encouragement is all it takes to keep most talkers going. So encourage the talker by paying attention to what he is saying. He's watching you for interest and approval. If he sees them, he'll open up.
• Encourage the speaker. When a little nudge is required to keep things moving, try to mirror the speaker's attitude about the subject. Repeat a

few of his words appreciatively or rephrase his sentiments. That will show him that he's getting through to you and will encourage him to go ahead.

• Clarify the thought. When the speaker shows signs of having had his say, take the initiative. Summarize what he's said. That sharpens the point for both of you and lays the groundwork for any further exploration of the subject that you may consider worthwhile.

• Pick a part from the whole. Here's where you move from passive listening to bringing out the points that interest you. From all that has been said, choose the portion you want to develop further. It's easy to discard the rest: Just don't respond to it.

• Ask questions. Finally, open your cross-examination. Ask leading, challenging questions. From here on, you will hear just what you ask for.

When you have followed through on all five steps, you will have listened the way the experts do. You have entered the unknown, explored it, chosen the most rewarding part of it, and zeroed in on the details that have interest or value for you. You've become a 20/20 listener!

The Habit of Asking Effective Questions

Winners recognize that one of the best ways of learning is to tap the brains of those who know what they don't.

But the ability to ask questions need not be confined to the gathering of information. It can be used to discover attitudes . . . arouse interest . . . put across a point of view . . . prove that you are listening . . . overcome antagonisms . . . help another crystallize his or her thinking . . . and on and on and on.

Here are some pointers on asking questions that should prove helpful in almost any kind of interrogatory situation.

• Begin with friendly, easily answered questions.
• Know what you want your questions to achieve. Are you asking for information? A favor? Clarification? Agreement?
• If you want to draw out another person, avoid questions that invite simple yes or no answers.
• Avoid getting too personal with your questions.
• Put your questions in terms the other person can readily understand.
• Give the person time to think before answering.

- Don't interrupt an answer to ask another question unless it is absolutely necessary.
- Avoid coming across like a cross-examiner.
- Don't ask questions that are merely designed to show your own knowledge.
- Try not to lead a speaker away from his or her own train of thought by your questioning.

The Habit of Excellence

Winners always do their best. They are driven to compete not only with others but with themselves. Toward this end, they follow a personal "zero defects" program, always trying to perform flawlessly. Even when they do not live up to their own high standards, the very attempt at perfection pays off in work of higher-than-average caliber.

They seldom settle for the first idea that occurs to them. They view every task, big or small, as a challenge to be met in a superior fashion. They may not do anything until they have drawn a mental list of three, four, or more possibilities, then eliminated those that appear most flawed. The remaining strategy is clearly the one to be adopted.

They anticipate problems. If one approach will require too much time, they opt for another. If they foresee a need for help, they check on the availability of other people before plunging in. If the effort to be invested in a job does not promise a sufficiently high payoff, they search for another solution.

They work hard, for it is results they are after, not leisure time. If an extra hour or day will yield what they are seeking, they are happy to spend it, knowing that there will be other hours and other days in which to do other things.

Above all, they want to experience the heady sense of achievement that doing a job extremely well gives them. For them, there is simply no substitute for that feeling.

The Habit of Thinking Logically

Winners think clearly. Realizing that many decisions are really the results of habit or instinct, not of true thought, they act as much as possible on the cold facts alone. The following suggestions should help you keep your own thinking on any problem within the bounds of logic.

• Avoid impulsive decisions. Don't arrive at a solution until you can trace how you arrived at it step by step.
• Assemble all the facts that have a bearing on the solution.
• Test every fact for its truth and relevance.
• Carefully examine any decision or solution that is too much in line with your own wishes. Life is simply not that easy.
• Challenge your first solution. Check every possible fact, whether it appears to favor or oppose your decision. You may have erred in judging it.
• Think "around" the subject. This gives you a cooling-off period, which serves as a defense against impulsive action.
• Be willing to follow the facts alone, even if the conclusion to which they lead is disagreeable.

The Habit of Admitting Errors

Winners admit their mistakes, for they know that no one can be right 100 percent of the time. If they are managers, they understand that they lose very little by confessing an error (unless it's a catastrophe) and stand to gain a great deal:

• Employee respect. By admitting your errors, you lend credibility to those occasions when you know you are right. Your people will be less apt to challenge your judgment if they know you are as tough on yourself as you are on them.
• Improved morale. The manager who does not set himself apart from his people by pretending to be infallible is almost certain to have a team working for him rather than a collection of individuals.
• Improved performance. One of the most effective ways to instruct others is by example. If you demonstrate that you value truth above excuses, that is what you will get from your people. Because if they know that you know that everybody, including yourself, is human, they will do their level best, no more perhaps, but definitely no less.

The Habit of Flexibility

Winners are never rigid in their thinking. They are always receptive to the ideas, suggestions, and criticisms of others. If you suspect that you are not, here are some ways to change your style.

• Do some part of your job differently. The more extreme the change, the better. Even the simple act of answering your own telephone, instead of leaving it to your secretary, will create new situations. It will make you more accessible to other people and hence to fresh thought.

• Read and absorb books, newspapers, magazine articles, or essays that express opinions diametrically opposed to your own.

• Broaden your circle of friends to include people outside of business and your normal social life. When you meet doctors, architects, teachers, and other nonbusiness types in a social situation, talk to them about their interests, not yours.

• Engage in a demanding extracurricular activity. Take an evening course in some subject that you have always wanted to know more about but never found the time to pursue. Become active in a volunteer organization, preferably with an organization with which you are unfamiliar. Try your hand at local politics. Involve yourself in any activity that takes you out of your immediate circle and exposes you to new experiences that can stimulate your thinking.

Cultivating a Habit

Admittedly, it is one thing to identify habits that ought to be developed into integral parts of our personalities and quite another thing to do so. Yet habits can be cultivated; indeed, they must be. And good habits are extremely desirable for a number of reasons.

First, they are time-savers. When you do something without thinking, you avoid the need to weigh alternatives and make decisions. In effect, you "automate" yourself.

Second, they help you conserve energy. There is little physical waste in a habit. Your body behaves efficiently because it has been programmed to do certain things in a reflex-action way.

Finally, habits are convenient. Imagine how exhausted you would be if you had none. Everything you do, from getting dressed in the morning to attending to the routine chores of your job to retiring in the evening, would be a burden. You would have to think about signing your name to a letter, consciously brake your car at a red light, concentrate on not bumping into people in the street—even remember to open doors before walking in or out of a building.

There are all kinds of habits, of course: good, bad, and innocuous. The same man may start his day off with a shower (good), followed by a cigarette and cup of black coffee (bad), then slide behind the wheel of his car, check the rearview mirror, turn the ignition key, and back out of his garage (innocuous).

It stands to reason that if you could consciously cultivate good habits, not only would you be able to become more efficient, delegating certain chores to your body that must now pass through your brain, but you could also crowd out your less desirable habits in the process.

There are ways to accomplish this. Here is a program that should help you form any habit you want.

Pinpoint What You Want. Before you can develop a habit, you must identify it. What, precisely, do you want to do? Speak better? Write more legibly? Read more? Stop smoking? Control your temper? Whatever it is, identify it.

But identification is not enough. You must also be sure you want it enough to take the pains it will require to develop it into a habit. Think it through until you are convinced in your own mind why it is important to you and what benefits you will derive from cultivating it. Perhaps it is a question of personal pride. It may increase your earning power. Possibly, it will enhance your professional standing. Whatever its importance to you may be, keep it firmly in mind.

Believe You Can Do It. When a person becomes genuinely convinced that he can do what he wants to do, there is no room in his mind for thoughts of failure. Assuming success, he goes after it with assurance. The secret behind this is simple: *You can think only one thought at a time.*

Want proof? For the next two minutes, try not to think of a white elephant. Go on. Try it. Close your eyes for 120 seconds and *don't* think of a white elephant.

Can't do it? Nobody can.

There is only one way not to think about it. That is to think of something else. You can think of only one thing at a time.

Think success and you leave no room for thinking failure. Act on the assumption that you can do what you set out to do, and you're on your way.

Take One Step at a Time.   Just as you can think only one thought at a time, so you can perform only one act at a time. Keeping yourself going boils down to keeping yourself going through your next thought and your next act: your next five minutes, your next hour, your next day.

Looking at it from the other point of view, it means not yielding to the impulse to turn aside and quit. These impulses come one at a time. You overcome them *one at a time.*

Suppose you want to develop the habit of giving words their full value when pronouncing them. You tend to slur words so that they sound like this: comin', wouldn', su'stantial. You vow that for the next five minutes you will consciously pronounce every letter of every word you say. Your lips work harder than they've ever worked before. Your tongue assumes strange positions. It's a great effort, but for five minutes you do indeed speak clearly. Next time, you can shoot for ten minutes.

The Chinese say, "The longest journey begins with the first step." This is the step that turns you in the direction you want to go and gets you started.

During World War II, a group of men—isolated, cut off from supplies— was defending an island in the Pacific. Stricken by malaria, threatened by air attacks, the men knew they could not hold out. But each night they voted on the question, "Should we hold out one more day?" Every night they voted yes. Eventually they were rescued. They had fought off surrender one day at a time.

One minute at a time, one hour at a time, one day at a time—one step at a time—will get you from where you are to where you want to be.

Put Yourself on the Spot.   When Jack Dempsey fought Carpentier at Boyle's Thirty Acres in New Jersey, a boxer in one of the preliminary bouts was a fellow who was written off as a ringman of little promise. The truth was that he had hurt his hands, and a boxer with brittle hands is not for the big time.

Unless, of course, he does something about them. This is precisely what this man did, because he had decided to become heavyweight champion of the world. He wanted this enough to do what he had to do to get there. He bought two rubber balls and put them in his pockets. Day after day he took these balls, one in each hand, and squeezed them—for five minutes at a time when he had the chance, for fifteen minutes when he could, for longer if the opportunity came, always persistently. At the same time he worked regularly at punching the heavy bag, lightly at first, then harder and harder as his hands became stronger.

When he decided that his hands could take it, he put himself on the spot. He signed up for a professional bout—and won. He added to his exercises, not only strengthening his hands but building his whole frame. Now he put himself on the spot again. He fought an opponent higher in the ratings—and won again.

He went on with his career, putting himself on the spot with the leading contenders for the title and disposing of them in turn. In 1926 he defeated Dempsey for the heavyweight crown. He defeated him again in the return match and retired as the undefeated champion.

Unless a person exposes himself to defeat periodically, as Gene Tunney did, he cannot prove to himself and the world that he is a champion.

As you pursue the habit you want, you can give youself that extra test periodically by putting yourself on the spot. You strengthen your willpower by creating situations in which you have to call on it for extra effort.

It's important to involve others, too, for the very human desire to save face is a powerful motivator. Tell your spouse or a friend that you have decided to make an extra effort to speak clearly at all times and that you are sticking your neck out by going on record. Rather than fail in their eyes, you will exert all your powers to live up to your announced goal. At the same time, you are creating allies who will help you police yourself.

Get the Habit. Do anything once, and you will do it more easily the second time. Do it twice, and the third time you will do it still more easily. Keep on doing it and you will find yourself repeating it without any conscious effort. You will be doing it automatically.

William James put it this way:

> The great thing in all education is to make our nervous system our ally instead of our enemy.
>
> For this we must make automatic and habitual, as early as pos-

sible, as many useful actions as we can, and as carefully guard against growing into ways that are likely to be disadvantageous.

In the acquisition of a new habit, or the leaving off of an old one, we must take care to launch ourselves with as strong and decided an initiative as possible.

Never suffer an exception to occur until the new habit is securely rooted in your life. Seize the very first possible opportunity to act on every resolution you make, and on every emotional prompting you may experience in the direction of the habit you aspire to gain.

To "make our nervous system our ally" is simple. We do the things that take us toward our goal over and over until it becomes easier to do them than to do any of the things that would divert us from what we really want. Just as repeated treks wear permanent pathways in the wilderness, so repeated actions wear deeper and broader traces in the brain.

Says James: The drunkard excuses himself for every fresh dereliction by saying, "I won't count this time." Well, *he* may not count it, but it is being counted nevertheless. Down among the nerve cells and fibers the molecules are counting it, registering and storing it up to be used against him when the next temptation comes. Nothing we ever do is, in strict scientific literalness, wiped out.

This has its good side as well as its bad one. As we become drunkards by so many separate drinks, so we become saints and experts by so many separate acts and hours of work.

In short, habits are self-reinforcing. Consciously do today what you want to do unconsciously tomorrow and eventually you will. It will happen imperceptibly at first, getting easier along the way. Then, one bright day, you will catch yourself in the act—doing automatically what you've longed to do.

Congratulations! You've got the habit.

6

Make the Time You Need

You won't find it in your wallet or your bank account. You can't borrow it. You can't work harder to earn more of it. And you certainly can't hoard it. In fact, all you can do with it is spend it.

It's time, of course, the universal coin of achievement, equally available to all.

Robert Ripley, the "Believe It or Not" man, once pointed out: "A plain bar of iron is worth $5. This same bar of iron, made into horse-shoes, is worth $10.50. If made into needles, it is worth $355. If made into pen knife blades, it is worth $3,285, and if turned into balance springs for watches, that identical bar of iron becomes worth $250,000."

The same is true of time. Some people can turn an hour into horse-shoes; others can turn it into needles. A smaller number know how to change it into knife blades. But only a few have learned how to trans-form a golden hour into true-tempered watch springs.

The Fifty-seven-Week Year

Most of us coast haphazardly through our days, relying on "crisis energy" and last-minute scrambling to get our jobs done. We dissipate our time capital with a recklessness we would never tolerate in our handling of money matters.

How about you? Can you honestly say that you are using your time in the most fulfilling, profitable way? At day's end, can you look back with satisfaction on a succession of accomplishments?

If you can honestly answer these questions with an unqualified yes, congratulations! Turn to the next chapter; there is nothing here for you.

If, however, you find yourself shaking your head and admitting that your minutes, hours, and days seem to glide wastefully by, read on. For while there is no way of trapping a minute and saving it for future use, there are scores of ways to use each passing minute so effectively that it does the work of two. A double-duty minute here, a tested shortcut there, and you will soon find the extra hours for which you have searched so long.

By mastering the following techniques and tips, you can increase your working-time capital by hundreds of hours annually.

Suppose you could save just two hundred hours—that's five forty-hour weeks—a year. What could you do with them? Or put another way, what *couldn't* you do with five extra weeks each year?

Time-check Yourself

In our hearts, most of us consider ourselves pretty efficient. But we are seldom called upon to prove it. The truth is, few people really know how they spend their time. Do you?

Try this little experiment. Write out as clearly as you can how you think you spend a typical workday. Put it away in a sealed envelope. Then run a time check on yourself for a couple of weeks. Jot down the time spent at various activities: traveling to and from work, reading and dictating letters, answering the telephone, attending meetings, and so on. The appropriate categories can be made up to suit your personal routine. After two weeks compare your lists. It's ten to one you end up slightly red-faced.

You are not alone. We all tend to idealize aspects of ourselves, including our accomplishments. A time check is one of the best ways to identify what we are really doing with the hours at our disposal.

Next, evaluate your use of time. Review your work pattern step by step and challenge each step with the simple question, "Why is this done?" Chances are you'll uncover needless details and some plain foolishness. How many of the time-consuming activities on your time check have to be done at all? Usually there will be several hours in the week spent doing things that can be cheerfully discontinued with no loss to anyone. How does your allocation and expenditure of time relate to important goals? Chances are the match is pretty poor. Major goals may be getting two hours a week of attention, for example, while inconsequential ones are eating up ten hours. Look for ways of reallocating your time to important projects.

Build Your Day Around "Core" Activities

If you stop to consider how your workday is spent, in all probability you will find that much of it is devoted to just a few activities: reading, writing or dictating, telephoning, and talking to people in person. Because these four major activities usually take place in a haphazard way, valuable time is frequently wasted in looking for things, making the mental "switch" from one activity to another, backtracking, and so on.

Try organizing your day around these basic duties. Set aside one period of time exclusively for making telephone calls, another for dictating letters and memos, a third for reading, a fourth for personal interviews. Of course, you will have to make allowances for the unexpected, but by segmenting your day you will almost surely get more done and with a minimum of conflict.

Another trap that many of us fall into is the temptation to linger over responsibilities that we particularly enjoy while neglecting other, more demanding, tasks. One woman, for example, may actually like to sign her mail because it requires no great thought, no decision-making ability, no risk taking. But the good time manager reduces the number of routine tasks he attends to and increases the number of tough jobs he tackles.

Trim the Fat from Your Workday

If you could somehow cut down on the idle chatter, pointless telephone calls, unproductive personal visits, and so on that fill your working hours, you might be amazed to learn how many minutes you literally throw away at work. Nobody is totally innocent; we all waste time.

But we have an ace in the hole. We can always learn to do better. Here are five quick time-savers you can implement immediately.

Keep Standing. When visitors or associates drop by unannounced simply to chat, be pleasant but get on your feet and stay on them. Once you both sit down, you may be in for some time killing that throws your entire schedule off.

Keep Telephone Conversations Short. When you initiate the call, tell your story in a few words, always pleasantly, with an opportunity for the other party to reply quickly.

Limit Meetings to Thirty Minutes. You can usually accomplish much more in a half-hour discussion, with a carefully planned agenda, than in an unstructured meeting lasting one or more hours.

Write Short Letters. If most letters were reduced by half, they would be twice as effective. At first it takes a little time to plan such a letter, but with practice it becomes an automatic reflex. Tell your reader in the first sentences exactly what he wants to know, just as a reporter tells his news story in the first lead lines. Avoid winding up, like a pitcher delivering a ball, with a whole paragraph acknowledging receipt of the inquiry. Jump right into the news the reader is looking for.

Work Rapidly. Strangely enough, the rapid worker is usually more accurate than the slow, steady one, perhaps because his concentration is deeper. Outstanding bank tellers, for example, perform most effectively when they are working fast at their own rhythms, alertly and accurately paying out money, often in large amounts, to a steady line of customers. You may find that you work best when you move quickly from doing one task to another without allowing your attention to wander. And the confidence you gain from such competence increases your momentum.

Get Rid of Clutter

The time killer called clutter is usually the direct result of lack of self-discipline. You permit your desk to become a catchall for outdated papers of every description: mountains of old correspondence, cartoons yellowing with age, magazines never referred to, forgotten advertisements, half-finished crossword puzzles, old receipts, outdated manuals, vintage Christmas cards—these are just some of the papers that add confusion to our lives.

Except for canceled checks and old receipts (which belong in an expanding envelope against the day you figure out your income tax), this clutter is a time murderer, for it forces you to spend hours every month searching for the papers you do need.

It has been estimated that 90 percent of an individual's business and personal papers are worthless. Get rid of them.

Sound ruthless? So's a clock!

Don't Dwell on Ancient History

Analyze the last ten decisions you made, the last ten reports or letters you wrote, the last ten conversations you held over the telephone or in person. Of those thirty items, it's a rare person indeed who won't find that at least fifteen were past oriented.

Granted, the past cannot be ignored. But it cannot be changed either. To the extent that you can learn from what has happened and need to know what has happened in order to make decisions in the present and future, by all means review the past. But don't worship it. The more past oriented the data you accumulate, the less time is available to you to study current situations.

Don't Spend Dollar Time on Penny Jobs

Bob Shaw was a junior executive in an electronics firm. One day his department head called a top-level meeting to hammer out some fundamental points of company policy. The meeting, scheduled for nine A.M. sharp, came to order precisely on time, but not a sign of Bob, who had a report to give.

A hurried phone call to Bob's home elicited this explanation from Mrs. Shaw: It was their son's birthday, and Bob had dashed downtown to pick up some streamers for the party that was to be held later in the day.

When a somewhat breathless Bob arrived at the meeting at 9:20, he was stunned to find the conference room smothered under what seemed miles of streamers.

"There are ten dollars' worth of streamers here," his department head explained. "And that's less than a twentieth of the amount of money you've cost the company by wasting your own time and the time of the other people here. To buy a dollar's worth of streamers for your boy's birthday, you spent over three dollars of your own time. That's bad management." A chagrined Bob Shaw came away from that meeting with a new respect for the value of time.

A salesperson who averages a commission of twenty dollars per sales call and takes a half-hour coffee break is drinking a twenty-dollar cup of coffee. A woman who earns eight dollars an hour spends forty dollars a month if she takes just fifteen minutes a day to drive her kids to school. If your time is worth fifty dollars a day, it costs you fifty cents just to run down the block for a newspaper.

So before you undertake any job, figure out what the result will be worth. Then estimate your time cost. Is the result worth it? If it isn't, either eliminate it or delegate it.

Skip the Formalities

Falsely believing that the only approved way of doing things is the formal way, some people will draft a letter or a memo, have it typed, correct it, then have it retyped when all they really want to do is pass along some information or ask a simple question. But why waste all that time (yours and your secretary's) when you can pick up the telephone or settle matters face to face in a few moments? As in virtually everything else, common sense is a reliable guide here. Before choosing the bureaucratic paper-producing path, see if you can't attain the results you want by simply using your voice.

Cut Off Long-winded Visitors

If you're not careful, business callers can waste a lot of your time. Here are five ways to keep such visits by outsiders brief and to the point.

• While your visitor is talking to you, listen closely and take notes so that he knows you are getting his story. Tell him, "I understand. I'm going to have Mr. Smith or Miss Jones take care of this for you." Then take the visitor to the other person and explain the situation from your notes.
• If you know a visitor is a long talker, schedule his visit immediately before some event which will give you an iron-clad reason for curtailing the visit (an appointment, a scheduled meeting which you must attend, or a waiting vehicle).
• If another person routinely handles your visitors, have him located near you. Drop in for just a moment during each visit to see what the call is about. That way, the visitor knows he is getting your personal attention and will be less likely to insist on seeing you exclusively.
• Schedule visits consecutively in one time period, not scattered throughout the day. The presence of other people waiting will often prompt visitors to shorten their stays. And by seeing one person right after another, you avoid time-wasting interruptions in the middle of other work.

• Review the visitors you've seen over the past few months. If the record indicates a pattern of too much time spent on certain types of visits, be firm in cutting down their length and number.

Use Form Letters

Realizing how much time he wasted annually writing the same few basic letters, a New York businessman had a pad of notepaper printed as follows:

Gentlemen:

I'm enclosing payment (   ); returning merchandise
for exchange (   ) or credit (   ); requesting samples (   )
or literature (   ).

Sincerely,

If anything further was necessary, he merely added a postscript.

Depending on your own particular needs and business-letter-writing pattern, some such similar form letter could save you hours every month.

Police Your Reading Time

Because the printed word is multiplying at an ever-increasing rate, nobody, but *nobody*, can keep up with all the reading he or she would like to do. To keep from falling too far behind, consider these suggestions.

• If you read more than one newspaper a day, cut down. Concentrate on the paper that gives the most complete coverage. By ruthlessly eliminating repetitious reading (most newspapers cover the identical major stories) you create time for additional reading that can yield fresh, valuable information.

• Read news magazines. You'll find that they do a creditable job of boiling down important news and give top coverage and perspective.

• Scan news summaries before hunting through your paper for interesting items.

• Check book reviews to determine those books you want to buy and read in full.

Let the Postman Run Your Errands

Do you find legwork eating into your time? For pennies, you can still hire the most reliable messenger in the world—Uncle Sam. He'll pay your bills; make bank deposits; deliver packages; get you train, plane, and ship schedules; bring you announcements of civic activities; pick up theater tickets; deliver magazines and books to your doorstep; hand you government publications and the answers to detailed questions on social security, veterans' benefits, income tax; dig up copies of birth certificates and other legal papers; even help you shop.

Where to Find Extra Time

It is one thing to do the things you must do in less time, but quite another to do more things. There are still just twenty-four hours in a day. Where is the additional time for hobbies, friends, family, and self-improvement to come from?

Here are some rich veins of time that you can mine for the extra hours you need for extra achievement.

Get Up a Little Earlier. One chief executive is always at his desk by eight A.M. Free from interruptions, he can plan his day, go over papers, and make the decisions that affect his firm's offices around the globe. By the time his vice-presidents arrive for work, a drift of memos has usually settled over their desks. He is an outstanding example of the person who purposely rises earlier than absolutely necessary in order to get things done.

Why not emulate him? You needn't rise at the crack of dawn; merely set your alarm to ring twenty or thirty minutes earlier than is your custom and use the extra time for reading, attending to your garden, pursuing a course of study, listening to music, or whatever *you* want to do.

Your Evenings. How much time do you have at your disposal from the moment you arrive home from work until bedtime? Four hours? Five? Six? How do you spend them? You eat, of course. Read the paper. Watch some television, perhaps. How about your family? Do you share some time with them? You should. Then there's you. An hour or two a night invested in study, for fun or job advancement, can give you that

"I'm going places" feeling. Be a bit more selective about the TV programs you watch and save precious time for your self-improvement goals. The TV page of your local newspaper gives you a brief synopsis of shows and permits you to check off those you want to see. Avoid the hit-and-miss approach.

Weekdays and Holidays.   Not counting your annual vacation, you have an incredible total of more than one hundred days off each year—well over three months of your very own! Sure, sleep a little later now and then; it will do you good. But put that treasure trove of time to use. In addition to indulging your taste for golf, fishing, or tennis, and to taking the family out and joining in community enterprises, you have over three months to learn your profession or business more thoroughly, to develop new skills and hone old ones.

Travel Time.   Even the minutes it takes you to get to your job can be put to work. If you are only half an hour from your office or plant, your morning travel alone adds up to 125 hours a year. Since we are often freshest in the morning, why not use that time to rehearse a presentation, think out an idea, plan the week's schedule? At day's end, when you're at low ebb, read the paper, clean out your briefcase, or just doze.

There may be other travel time in your day. If you keep appointments, use minutes in transit to think out ideas, catch up on quick reading chores, mull over your day so far, and jot down memory joggers to yourself.

If you ride in a car pool, you have a golden opportunity to pick the brains of your fellow passengers.

Waiting Time.   A business appointment is over sooner than you expected . . . you miss your train . . . the person you've come to see is tied up. It all adds up to usable time during which you can read a few pages, draft a letter, plan your evening, make a phone call, or just plain think.

Eating-alone Time.   On those days when you eat alone, you can have extra dessert in the form of spare minutes. How about visiting a library; attending to those little, but time-consuming, chores usually reserved for after five P.M.; or examining sections of the newspaper you normally skip (they could open a whole new world to you)?

Time, like a river, is constantly rushing by. It cannot be captured, bottled, or stored for future use. Once passed, it is gone forever. Bear its transient nature in mind and you will find your attitude toward it shifting from that of a spendthrift to that of a miser. You will be in good company, for the doers of the world—who also tend to garner the world's rewards—are all stingy with their time.

They also have something else in common. They recognize that, as space is the dimension through which things move, so time is the dimension in which things get done, and they are achievement oriented. You should be too. We will now consider specific techniques.

7

How to Boost Your Personal Productivity

Any machine that performed as inefficiently as a human being would be yanked off the market. For absolutely nobody works at anywhere near his or her full potential. Most of us, it has been estimated, chug along at 15 to 20 percent of our true capacities. During periods of stress, we may increase our performance coefficient fractionally, but generally we work on only a few cylinders. To be sure, an occasional da Vinci or Einstein appears on the scene and dazzles the world with a sustained performance that may represent 30, 40, even 50 percent of what he is really capable of, but the average mortal bumbles along, trailing clouds of inefficiency behind him.

While there is no known way for a person even to approach 100 percent of his potential on the job (and if he did, he would without doubt be summarily lynched by his colleagues), there are a number of ways in which he can improve his productivity dramatically.

If you can honestly say that you are accomplishing everything you should, you are a rare bird indeed. But if, like the vast majority of us, you entertain the gnawing suspicion that something is awry with your personal productivity, it may be time for some serious self-examination, for if we do not achieve what we are capable of achieving, the weakness almost always has its roots in some personal failing. Two of these weaknesses in particular warrant discussion: habits and attitudes.

Bad Work Habits

There are certain on-the-job practices that are guaranteed to block accomplishment. If any of the following sound familiar, they'll need attention:

Procrastination. Faced by a large or complex job, procrastinators will find a dozen little things to attend to before tackling it. Faced by a little job, they will put it off because "it will only take a few minutes." Either way, they do nothing.

Lack of Planning. You get wherever you are going a lot faster if you know your destination. Basic stuff? Perhaps. But most people muddle through ineffectively because they have never pinpointed in their own minds precisely what they have to do. Poor results are a foregone conclusion.

Indecision. This habit is the result of either lack of pertinent information on which to base a decision or lack of confidence in one's ability to think through a problem. By putting off a decision, postponers are really demonstrating their desire for someone else to decide for them. It goes without saying that they are dismissed out of hand at promotion time.

Knee-jerk Reflexes. The habit of responding to new circumstances in old ways may be comfortable initially, but by its very nature it is anti-creative and counterproductive. New problems demand fresh solutions. And the only way to arrive at fresh solutions is through innovative thinking.

Harmful Attitudes

Habits are merely the more visible signs of attitudes. If you are to rid yourself of bad habits, it is necessary to attack the substructures on which they rest. Among the most harmful are the following:

Mediocrity. While no one consciously believes that he or she is dedicated to just getting by, you are guilty of this attitude if you customarily settle for the first idea that comes to mind, accept the status quo without question, take dangerous shortcuts in the name of expediency, never deviate from "the book."

Boredom. Any job loses its excitement with the passage of time. But workers who take no steps to find something interesting in what they do or to inject their own excitement into it are dooming themselves to below-par performance.

Discouragement. Some people cannot snap back when they are thrown for a loss. Was an idea of theirs criticized? They'll never come up with another one. They didn't solve that problem immediately? What's the use of trying? However, no one goes through life chalking up one success after another. Doers do, despite setbacks.

Lack of Self-motivation.   You cannot always rely on others to provide the propelling force you require to get things done. They have their own needs, problems, and responsibilities. Somehow, you must learn to trigger enthusiasm and action within yourself. You must cultivate a certain pride in the caliber of your work and an eagerness to accomplish that enables you to overcome discouragement, boredom, and assorted disappointments.

Awareness of the habits and attitudes that hamper accomplishment is important, for once you know what they are, you can take steps either to correct them, or to eliminate them from your character. But this knowledge is only half the battle. Next, and equally important, you must understand, and do, the things upon which solid achievement is based.

Start Your Day Off Right

How you start your day often determines how much you will accomplish, how well you will get along with others, and how you will feel by five P.M. Three specific steps you can take to guarantee getting off to a good start are:

Make Yourself Want to Get Up.   Instead of dwelling on the discouraging things you have to face, concentrate on the most enjoyable thing you have to do that day. You'll find it a lot easier to get out of bed.

Anticipate Minor Decisions.   "What should I wear?" "Where's the Davis report?" "Anybody see my commuter ticket?" Petty decisions and minor frustrations can waste time, frazzle nerves, and easily ruin a morning. Solution: Decide the night before what you will wear, what you need to take to the office or your place of business, and lay everything out before going to bed. In the morning you'll have surprisingly few problems!

Have a Good Breakfast.   Contrary to popular opinion, the cigarette-and-black-coffee routine is not a time-saver in the long run. It only postpones hunger and meanwhile irritability.

Take Physical Inventory

To a large degree, how well you function on the job depends on how you feel. Almost anything, from tight shoes to poor ventilation, can reduce your personal productivity and adversely affect your performance. Because you work best when your environment is conducive to achievement, the few moments needed to take physical inventory of yourself and your work area can be worthwhile. Here is a checklist that enables you to see if you are physically prepared to tackle a major job. Before diving in, make sure that you can honestly check every "yes" box below:

	YES	NO
Am I dressed comfortably for the work I have to do?	☐	☐
Am I well rested?	☐	☐
Have I eaten properly?	☐	☐
Is the temperature set for optimum comfort?	☐	☐
Is the lighting adequate?	☐	☐
Have I eliminated all distractions?	☐	☐
Do I have all the tools and equipment to do the job?	☐	☐

If all your answers are in the affirmative, you can be sure that you are physically prepared to get to work. If your answer to any of the questions is negative, correct the situation before going any further.

How to Get "Hot"

No person's body temperature stays at exactly 98.6 degrees Fahrenheit. The variations in your daily temperature mirror your basal metabolism, the complex process by which your body "stokes its furnace." This fluctuation of an individual's working efficiency coincides with the variations in his or her body temperature. In other words, we are most mentally alert when our body temperature is high-normal and least so when our temperature is low normal. This is why some people are at their best in the morning; others, in the afternoon; still others, in the evening.

If you want to find out your own best times for work, try taking your temperature hourly during your waking hours. You will find some period during which it is highest; these are your peak hours for creative, demanding work.

But suppose you discover that although you need to be in top mental shape from nine to eleven A.M., your temperature peak is four to six P.M.? Is there anything you can do about it? Fortunately, there is.

Your body temperature may be coaxed higher either by a long, hot shower or bath or by exercise or calisthenics. Once achieved, body temperature stays high, changing your day's entire cycle. Over a period of time (which varies with the individual), the body may actually be "retrained" to achieve its highest temperature at the desired time.

Set Priorities

The logic of this is simple. You can do only one thing at a time. If you try to do that one thing while worrying about the other jobs you can't do at the same time, you will take longer on the job you are doing and fall further behind. So always list the jobs you must do in the order of their importance and tackle them one at a time. Forget the others until you have finished the one you're working on.

In the office or in your pocket, a daily calendar is essential. If a new job has to be started or followed up next Wednesday, note this on Wednesday's page and forget about it until then. If a letter has to be answered on Thursday after you get some needed information, do *not* keep the letter on your desk while you wait a couple of days for the information. Slip it between your calendar pages or, if you have many such letters, into a Thursday folder. You'll spot it Thursday and, if you haven't received the information, it will remind you to follow up.

In short, put everything you can on a timetable. Note it down and forget it until the right time comes.

Establish Time Limits

After you decide the importance of the tasks before you, set time limits for their accomplishment. Tell yourself, for example, that you will definitely have those blueprints ready by Tuesday, read those reports before lunch, and draft that memo before the day is over.

When you set time limits, you challenge yourself. Everyone cherishes a certain image of himself and will do virtually anything to sustain that self-image. Almost everyone's self-image includes a sense of honor. We like to believe we can be counted on. By establishing a time limit in which to accomplish something, we are in a sense challenging our own good opinion of ourselves. In order to meet the challenge, we summon all our capabilities. It amounts to saving face in front of yourself, and it is a powerful incentive.

Time limits also alert your body to the task to be completed. Sit in an easy chair and your muscles relax. You breathe slowly, and your pulse beats at a normal rate. But if you get up with the intention of lifting that easy chair, your muscles, anticipating the job before them, flex and tighten; you breathe faster in order to deliver the extra oxygen your body requires for work; your pulse quickens as your heart pumps more blood to all parts of your body. Many other subtle physiological changes take place. In the same way, the knowledge that a certain task must be accomplished by a specified time alerts your body to prepare itself for the job at hand. Even if the assignment is mental, writing a report for example, your body responds by sending more blood, and oxygen, to your brain.

Finally, by establishing definite deadlines you are being affirmative. "If you think you can, you can," it has been said. When you say to yourself, "I'll have that presentation whipped into shape by Monday," you are really declaring your ability to prepare the presentation within the designated time. And it's always easier to do something when you are convinced that you can do it.

Keep Your Deadlines Realistic

The best-laid plans, however, do not always work out. Allowances must be made for unforeseen obstacles, interruptions, and necessary changes in plan. Your deadlines, therefore, should be reasonable, for if they are not and you fail to meet them, you risk frustration and loss of confidence. To avoid either pitfall, bear the following guidelines in mind before you set your time limits.

• Allow sufficient time for fact gathering. Many tasks require specialized information: Reports must be read, people consulted, telephone calls made. Take these preliminary steps into consideration when establishing your deadline.

• Don't forget the tools you will need. Whether your task calls for paper clips or power tools, remember the time it will take to beg, borrow, or buy the proper equipment.

78 MOVING ON UP

• Beware of costly interruptions. Telephone calls, visitors, conferences, little emergencies—all these can throw a schedule out of kilter. Unless you have already found Shangri-La, make allowances for these petty time thieves.

• Prepare for variations in your energy supply. We all experience bursts of energy as well as short circuits. On a day when you know you're clicking, you can shave your deadlines, confident that you will meet them. On off days, give yourself some leeway.

By keeping your time limits realistic, you will avoid the doer's arch-enemy—deadline jitters—that unreasoning jumpiness that can paralyze your faculties and triple the difficulty of any job. A deadline is like a suit: Too tight or too loose, it doesn't allow you to show yourself at your best; but carefully tailored, it flatters, builds confidence, and is supremely practical.

One Secret of Getting a Big Job Done

In a now-classic experiment conducted by the Psychology Department of Columbia University, a group of volunteers had one-pound weights suspended from their index fingers. They were instructed to crook the finger, thus lifting the weight, for as long as they possibly could. Only when they were certain that they could not budge the weight were they to signal the psychologist in charge.

Some of the volunteers were able to lift the weight one hundred times or more. But sooner or later, each reached his own individual point of total exhaustion, a point where his finger felt paralyzed and incapable of any further motion. None of the subjects could see any of the others, and as each succumbed in turn, the psychologist hurried over to him and whispered something in his ear.

In every single case, *without exception*, the volunteers were able to lift the weight many more times after listening to the psychologist. Some were able to lift it more than twenty times past the point they were initially convinced represented complete exhaustion. Several subjects bettered their original performances by almost 30 percent.

What magic phrase did the psychologist utter? Simple. What he whispered was this: "From this point on, I will give you a dollar for every time you lift the weight."

A dollar bill for merely crooking the index finger! Suddenly, fingers came to life. The weights moved swiftly, firmly. Why? Because nothing is better geared to extract that last ounce of effort out of a human being than a reward or the prospect of one.

What does this mean to you? Very simply, that if, as you check on your progress through a big job, you reward yourself as each subgoal along the way is reached, you will lay the psychological groundwork for additional achievement. It is precisely when we think that our last effort has taken everything out of us—imagination, perseverance, energy—that we desperately need a shot in the arm. Rewards provide this, They excite us. They give us immediate pleasure. They provide tangible proof that we are getting somewhere. And they help make a game out of what is essentially a serious business.

So an integral part of attacking any big job is to set, in advance, "reward points," those places along the road to completion of the task where you will consciously pause and treat yourself to something because you have earned it. Since only you know what counts for you, set your own reward goals—a cigar, dinner out, a weekend trip to the big city. It will pay off without fail and help get that big job done!

Put Yourself on a Thirty-Day Cycle

Most of us are willing enough to keep an eagle eye on others in order to see that they do not waste their time or energy on the job. But when it comes to policing ourselves, we are understandably lenient.

But such leniency isn't always desirable, particularly when you consider that, if you are a manager, you are a model for subordinates. So, to get more done and serve as a good example for others, try this.

At the beginning of a new month, establish your work goals for the next thirty days. Keep them realistic, but not easy. At the end of this period of probation, see what you have accomplished. Judge yourself as sternly as you would someone else. In between, keep your eye on how much ground you are covering or how much more must be done before month's end. Concentrate on the quality of the work you are doing rather than the quantity.

In a relatively short time you will find that you have formed the habit of thinking of the month as a whole, not as thirty vaguely related periods of time, Then, even if one day's output is disappointing, you won't feel dejected. Instead, you will see it for what it really is—a minor setback in the bigger thirty-day picture.

Have You Checked Your Priorities Lately?

Ironically, many a hardworking manager gets buried under his job because he's working hard on the wrong things. To determine what is most important at any given time is one of his toughest challenges. But the person who continually meets this challenge is almost certain to stay on top of his job.

The truth is that the things that are most important today may be among the least important tomorrow. How do you determine the ever-shifting priorities of your work?

One manager does it this way: At a monthly meeting with his people, he invites them to give their estimates of the most important problems the department faces. Their answers reflect the priorities in their own areas of responsibility. He then weighs their opinions against his.

This accomplishes two things. First, he spots projects that are being overrated and can take steps to place them where they belong on the scale of importance. He also pinpoints projects that are being delayed because they have been mistakenly put at the bottom of the priorities list.

He thus accomplishes what every manager must accomplish if he is to do his job: He keeps the partnership between himself and his people alive and vibrant. And he learns from those who are closest to the jobs at hand. A person like that is ready for a bigger job.

Learn to Delegate

It's a law! The more avenues of escape you create for a pressure, the less that pressure can build up.

This is particularly true of on-the-job pressures. If you have a deadline to meet or too many places to be at one time or too much responsibility to shoulder, an excellent safety valve is delegation. Whenever possible, reduce the pressure on yourself by finding ways and means to spread it around. Answering the following questions will help you do just that. In each case bear in mind the particular pressure involved.

- "What must be done that can be handled by others?" You will be pleasantly surprised to find how dispensable many of your functions are.
- "Who can do what jobs?" Your secretary? A subordinate? A free-lancer? Another department? Don't pass the buck, of course, but don't be afraid to locate qualified helpers either.
- "Are there any mechanical aids that I can use?" Such time and energy savers may include the telephone, a dictating machine, a calculator, an electric typewriter, a copier, a computer, and power tools among others.
- "Who has had experience with this kind of job?" Identify those people and seek their advice. They may be able to save you a lot of backtracking, point out pitfalls, and help solve problems that are new to you but familiar to them. Drawing on the experience and expertise of others is an oft-overlooked form of delegation.

Avoid Delegation Traps

Question: What has five heads, ten arms, ten legs, and accomplishes very little?

Answer: A bad delegator who manages four people.

The manager who has the abilities of others to call upon is seriously shortchanging himself and his people if he doesn't take full advantage of them. Most of us could improve vastly in the area of delegation if we only recognized where we went wrong and took steps to correct our errors. Consider the following common traps; avoiding them can improve your own performance as a delegator and a manager.

Not Delegating Enough.   Managers, particularly new ones, find it almost painful to relinquish responsibilities. Faced with deadlines and pressures from above, the urge to "do it myself" and get it done is almost irresist-ible. But it's an urge at war with your basic responsibility as a manager, which is to get things done through others. If you allow yourself to be-come swamped by minutiae, you will not have sufficient time or energy to do your real work, namely, planning, controlling, and developing your people.

Not Communicating Effectively.   Delegation, by its very nature, is a form of communication. But not only must you make crystal clear to a subordinate what he is supposed to accomplish; you must encourage *him* to communicate with you. If you give the impression, for instance, that you will think less of him if he comes to you for advice or guidance, you are laying the foundation for a lesser performance than he is capable of.

Not Delegating Commensurate Authority. If you want an individual to do something, he needs the right amount of clout to get it done. If his job involves gathering information from others, for example, a memo to those he'll be contacting would probably help considerably. In all fairness, let him know the extent of his authority—what he can do as well as what he cannot do—lest he either underestimate or overestimate it, with consequent embarrassment to all concerned.

Not Allowing for Error. Managers who are reluctant to delegate usually have had one or more bad experiences—a botched job by a subordinate, criticism from above, ulcers. But the mistake is not in delegating work; it is in not allowing for error. Delegation involves risk, but if the risk is taken into consideration, it needn't end in disaster. Schedule checkpoints so that you can spot trouble early enough to take remedial action. Then use the error for what it is—a learning situation for the employee.

Delegating Beneath Potential. One reason for delegating is to "stretch" your people. Among other things, delegation is a training tool, or should be. So don't restrict your delegating only to those areas in which employees have experience or special knowledge. Assign jobs for which you discern potential in them and see if your faith is justified. They may prove even more valuable than you suspect.

Concentrate

Some days seem especially designed for goofing off. We arrive at the office full of high resolve, only to watch the minutes and hours dribble away unproductively. We look over the newspaper, check with our co-workers to see how things are progressing at their end of the shop, gaze out the window, decide that this might be a good time to rearrange our files. Before long, lunch is on the horizon; no point in settling down to serious work. And on and on and on . . . .

Yet, under pressure, we have all drawn upon special resources that have enabled us to perform at our optimum levels. Not the least of these resources is a singleness of purpose that allows us to drive out all thoughts that do not immediately contribute to the work at hand—in a word, concentration.

The key to concentration is learning to create this singlemindedness at will. The following steps will help.

Sell Yourself on the Benefits of Concentration. If you can charge the job you must do with highly emotional content, you will automatically increase your interest in, and hence, your attention to it. One way to do this is to view the job in intensely personal, even selfish, terms. By asking yourself "What's in it for me?" you will gain the necessary impetus to dive in with all your energy. Maybe the answer is, "I'll impress the boss." Perhaps it's "I'll be able to shoot up to the country with the family for a long weekend." Find the emotional reason for concentrating and you will soon persuade yourself to concentrate.

If that doesn't work completely, bolster your resolve by taking the opposite tack. Ask yourself, "What do I stand to lose if I don't buckle down?" It may mean having to work over the weekend, the loss of a big account, disgrace in your boss's eyes. Somewhere there is a built-in threat of loss in not concentrating, be it money, prestige, or time. Whatever it is, identify it and run scared.

Tune Out the World. Jean Kerr, the author of several best sellers and of the hit play *Mary, Mary*, is also the mother of five. How did she ever find the time and quiet in which to write? Simple. With pad and pencil she retreated to her car and parked several blocks from home, isolated from family, friends, and telephones. You may not be able to run away quite so completely, but there are a few steps you can take to ensure your privacy:

• Find a place to work inaccessible to others: an empty office, the public library, an attic room, the basement.

• Rearrange your lunch hour so that you're on the job when your co-workers are out eating and gain sixty minutes of golden silence.

• Eliminate the means of escape. Everyone has his or her own favorite method of avoiding work, and as we have noted, people are at their most ingenious in devising excuses for not tackling a chore. Get rid of temptation by *not* having a copy of your favorite magazine or newspaper within reach, by *not* placing your desk in front of a window with an interesting view, particularly of people, by *not* attempting serious concentration with someone else in the room, by *not* initiating any telephone calls unless absolutely necessary, by *not* trying to work under adverse conditions such as noise, heavy traffic, or a disorganized work area.

Let Your Interest Take Over. When you are interested in something, you have little, if any, difficulty concentrating on it. Indeed, the problem is often how to stop concentrating long enough to do less interesting things that need doing. Any ardent hobbyist can vouch for that.

But if it is true that interest stimulates concentration, it is also true that concentration stimulates interest. Concentration triggers interest, which triggers greater concentration, which triggers greater interest, and so on. The challenge is to get this cycle started. And the surefire way to set it in motion is by *forcing* yourself to concentrate at first. If you find your attention wandering, pull it back with a conscious effort. If it wanders ten times, pull it back eleven times. The human capacity for becoming interested will eventually take care of the rest.

There is no such thing as an uninteresting subject; there are only uninterested people who don't care enough to concentrate on it. To say that you can't concentrate on anything because you are not interested is to slam the door without giving yourself a chance. Concentrate—really concentrate—on what you are doing and human nature will do the rest. All you really need to do is set off the "interest mechanism" that is part of you. Here's how:

Arouse Your Curiosity. You were born with the instinct to be curious. It's as much a part of you as the need to breathe. Remember all the questions you asked as a child? Undoubtedly you have seen this penchant for posing questions demonstrated by your own children. If you find your concentration on a subject waning, ask yourself some questions about it. By thus fueling your curiosity, you will revive your interest-concentration-interest cycle.

Talk to an Expert. Have you ever noticed how much you enjoy talking about a subject in which you are interested? Maybe it's skin diving, jazz, sports cars, or politics, but once you get started, it's hard to stop. You undoubtedly take pleasure in talking to other people with the same interests. Their comments, questions, and excitement feed your own enthusiasm and make you even more interested. The more you learn about anything, the more you want to learn about it.

Think of a subject in which you would like to be more interested. To step up your enthusiasm, visit the library and take out three or four books on the subject. But don't read them in the traditional way. Instead, read only the introduction and first chapter of each. In all probability, this introductory matter will be devoted to a discussion of why the author believes the subject is important. Pay close attention to what he has to say; some of his enthusiasm is bound to rub off on you.

If you can actually speak to one or more experts in your own company or elsewhere, so much the better.

Get Involved. If you want to master a skill, don't be a passive spectator. Simply soaking up facts like a blotter isn't going to guarantee interest. Whenever possible, *do something* with the information you acquire. The simple act of taking notes at a meeting or lecture or while reading can do wonders. It forces you to make a definite response to the information before you. The moment you put your pen to paper, for that fleeting instant you have fixed your mind on the subject. Later, when you study your notes, you are challenged to understand, to interpret, to recall.

Your personal involvement is a proven interest builder that inevitably makes it easier for you to concentrate. Aristotle said it best: "You learn how to do things by doing the things you want to be able to do."

Concentration, in short, grows with practice. The more you prepare yourself, by selling yourself in the benefits, by tuning out the world, and by setting off your interest-concentration-interest mechanism, the easier you will find it to get down to brass tacks.

When to Memorize

Whether it's a complex oral report that you are slated to give or a simple fact that you want to check out, research indicates that you will probably engrave it more deeply into your mind if you memorize it between eight and ten A.M. The reason: At that time your nervous system has fewer new impressions. In the evening, efficiency and memory may drop by as much at 6 to 10 percent. Your retentive powers lose strength gradually from waking to retiring. Sunday seems to be the worst day for remembering, probably because we take things easiest then.

Pay Attention to Your Posture

Efficiency results from small as well as large factors. It's important, for example, when seated, to maintain a relaxed, unfatiguing posture, since poor posture diminishes the proper intake of air into the lungs and can even reduce mental alertness. To boost your efficiency through better posture, the experts advise:

• Always sit tall and well back into your chair. The base of the spine should extend several inches from the rear part of the chair, thus avoiding pressure upon the sensitive lower-back area and consequent interference with proper blood circulation.

• The chair seat should not extend so far forward as to exert pressure upon the blood vessels and nerves in the rear of the knee and lower thighs. Pressure here retards circulation to the feet and legs.

• The height of the seat should permit your feet to rest upon the floor or one ankle to be lightly crossed over the other. This posture is restful and comfortable and can be maintained without effort.

Three Efficiency-Improving Techniques

Want to get more things done—faster? Research has uncovered some fascinating techniques.

• Experiments at West Germany's Max Planck Institute indicate that in an eight-hour day, three spaced five-minute coffee breaks are more beneficial than one fifteen-minute break. The reason is that the first five minutes of a rest period give the most relaxation.

• Long Island University researchers have found that most people are more alert on their feet than when sitting down. Pacing back and forth can actually help you think better.

• Carefully controlled experiments show that in the exertion of physical labor, grunting and groaning on the job really increase your strength by as much as 5 percent!

Try a "Procrastination Drawer"

While there is a lot to be said in favor of attending immediately to paperwork, at least one executive has found deliberate procrastination a great energy saver. You may too. In his words:

I used to think I had to settle every matter that came up then and there. Struggling, straining, and devoting time to these individual situations, I found I often missed really important things. After a while, I concluded that many of these troubles and trivia were of no consequence whatsoever. So now I take such papers and toss them into a special "procrastination drawer." When the drawer fills, I go through it and find to my surprise and pleasure that 75 to 90 percent of the annoying and irritating problems have solved themselves! Sometimes, there's a miss. But it's the average that counts.

Build Victory on Victory

The inclination to relax and savor a particular achievement is very human, but it's bad psychology. When you have accomplished something really worthwhile—solved a tough problem, finished a demanding report, made a breakthrough of some kind—don't stop to celebrate. Go right on with your schedule. Tackle the next problem. After a victory you're brimming with confidence. Your enthusiasm, as well as your thought processes, is at concert pitch. This is precisely the time to confront your next most nagging task. Failure doesn't matter so much on the day of conquest because you're already successful. In this relaxed, confident frame of mind, you will probably make some headway on that toughie. And even if you don't, you're laying a solid foundation for future accomplishment.

Take Breaks to Recharge

You can be more effective on the job and save time in the long run by investing time in getting a fresh start. Sir Winston Churchill and President Harry Truman, both masters of the catnap, testified to its power to recharge energy. Bernard Baruch credited his ability to bring fresh thinking to a problem to his habit of relaxing on a park bench.

You may not be able to indulge in catnaps or leave your job and head for a park, but you can take the kind of breaks that will have the same beneficial results. Some ideas:

• A steaming cup of coffee at eleven A.M. or four P.M. can clear your mind for action and pep up your body. Dream a little while you sip. It's

the next best thing to forty winks. If coffee's not your cup of tea, try tea or your favorite soft drink.
• Gaze out a window for a few minutes. It is good for your eyes and a tonic for your brain.
• Take a few deep breaths and stretch. Sometimes we get drowsy simply because our bodies are oxygen starved. Fill those lungs with fresh air, loosen muscles with a good stretch, and snap out of that slump.
• Eat a candy bar. Sugar is an ace pepper-upper. Of course, if you are fighting a personal battle of the bulge or do not care for sugar, this may not be for you. But now and then, for a change of pace, munch.

Be Decisive

No matter how you earn your living, you must choose between alternative courses of action hundreds of times each year. Reluctance to make a choice sabotages action and, therefore, achievement. To acquire the habit of decisiveness, try these four rules:

• Decide the small things promptly. By getting them out of the way, you give yourself more time to think through the things that really count.
• Select your choices firmly. It will put iron into your resolution.
• Abandon all alternatives. Once your mind is made up, forget the other possibilities. They are ancient history. "What could have been" thinking is unproductive.
• Act upon your decision. Nothing really happens until you do something. So if you truly want to be decisive, you must carry out your decision through action. Don't be afraid to make a mistake. J. P. Morgan once defined a successful man as "a fellow who is right fifty-one times out of one hundred." Right or wrong, come to a decision promptly after weighing all pertinent factors. Whichever it is, it is almost always better than no decision at all.

Take Out Mistake Insurance

Everybody makes mistakes. And everybody occasionally has to face the prospect of changing course or undoing an error.
The best way to avoid being trapped by an error is to prepare in ad-

vance a second plan of action in case the first goes awry. There is nothing defeatist about such a plan. In fact, there are two major reasons for having a backup plan ready when a decision must be changed. First, the moment when a mistake is realized is almost always a time of pressure. And second, the knowledge that a move can be reversed promotes path-finding. The feeling that decisions may be irreversible tends to paralyze the decision-making process and to encourage timidity.

The best medicine, of course, is preventive medicine. But because preventive therapy is not always possible, a second-best medicine should be kept in the top drawer. This is the kind that dilutes the effects of a mistake, even though it may not prevent them entirely. This second type of therapy calls for making decisions that foresee the possibility of error or of changing circumstances. It means preparing for a possible change without obscuring the main goal.

It may help to go over these points as a regular part of your decision-making routine:

What can go wrong with this plan?

How serious would any error be?

What can be done to lessen the possible impact of a mistake?

Develop the habit of arming yourself with the answers to these three questions before implementing a decision, and you will enjoy the supreme peace of mind that comes with knowing that you carry "mistake insurance."

Ten Ways to Reduce Your Work Load

Your value to yourself and your employer is directly related to the amount of work you complete with dispatch. If you can recognize the obstacles standing between you and your work and develop techniques for hurdling them, you will automatically increase that value. Any one of the following techniques could dramatically raise your worth on the job.

• Arrange your work to dispose of those things that can be handled promptly. The remaining projects will appear less formidable if your work pile no longer looks like a hopeless task to tackle. Simple psychology.

• Next, concentrate on the tough or unpleasant jobs. Get them out of the way while you're relatively fresh. Don't invite discouragement by letting them accumulate.

• But stop wrestling with a problem that has you stymied. Put it aside and come back to it when your mood and mind have improved. Be careful, of course, not to postpone the task indefinitely.

• Keep work on top of your desk where it will haunt you. It will stand a better chance of getting done. Burying work keeps it out of sight and away from completion. (However, see "Try a 'Procrastination Drawer,'" page 86.)

• Develop shortcuts where possible. For instance, reply to a memo at the bottom of the memo page instead of dictating a formal answer. It will save both time and money.

• Learn to make certain decisions more quickly. "I'll let you know later" only means that investigating a situation or listening to a problem must be repeated when the decision is finally made. Decide when the problem is posed, however, and the job is done.

• Take time to communicate with others who may be interested or involved with you in a project. A few minutes spent at the start to explain something can save endless hours later by preventing misunderstandings or fuzzy instructions.

• Say no to some of the requests made of you. It's flattering to be asked to speak or to serve on a committee. But these invitations are also cruel demands upon your time and energy, neither of which is limitless.

• Examine your miscellaneous duties periodically. You may find that some of them are merely habits and can no longer be defended as necessary. Routine has an unbelievable power to intrude into productivity.

• Don't let your briefcase become a "griefcase." Develop a balanced way of life with outside interests and avenues for relaxation, for unless you enjoy good health and peace of mind, you cannot work well day in and day out.

Learn to Stop Work—Effectively

If a job is going to take an extended period of time, you're going to have to do it in parts. But what can you do to ensure that your second, third, and fourth sessions will be at least as productive as your first? The trick is to stop working in a way that will maximize the effort just made.

• Quit at a point of satisfaction, if possible, thereby associating the effort with gratification.

• End at some natural point of intermediate accomplishment—at a subgoal.

• Clarify or identify your frustration if you end without the success you desire. Get it down in writing. Give the frustration a good kickoff into your subconscious for nondirected attention.

• Put your work into such physical shape as will enable you to resume it promptly and easily. Take stock of your accomplishments. Summarize and draw conclusions. Put your working materials away in orderly condition. Avoid having to unravel knots when starting.

Don't Bang Your Head Against a Brick Wall

Problems have a stubborn habit of not immediately yielding to solutions. When that happens, people have an equally stubborn habit of persisting in their errors. They will try the same solution over and over, perhaps modifying it a bit here and there, but with the same doleful results. The final score is inevitable: problem, 1; people, 0.

To break this profitless circle, it is often the better part of valor to give up for a while and tend to other things. Why? Because when frustration sets in during a bout with a problem, it rapidly turns to irritation, then hostility, and finally stubbornness; then the whole mess starts over again. Perspective, good judgment, and productivity go out the window. We mutter to ourselves, "No blankety-blank machine [customer, employee, superior, policy, department] is going to get the better of me!" Our boiling point gets lower and lower, and soon we are sputtering away half of our energy and two-thirds of our intelligence while the problem continues to grow bigger and more unassailable in our minds.

By turning our attention elsewhere for a while, however, we impose a colling-off period on ourselves; we get the requisite time in which to regain our composure and self-confidence and give our subconscious a chance to wrestle with the problem on a more creative level. More often than not, when we return to the problem, the solution pops into our mind, almost uninvited, and we wonder why we were ever stymied in the first place.

So when a problem has you down, try to solve it by all means, but don't waste your time banging your head against a brick wall.

8

Sharpen Your Communications Skills

Have you even noticed that the people who get promoted tend to be articulate, both in person and on paper? It's more than mere coincidence. Much of the world's work is accomplished through words. We use them to inform, explain, propose, persuade, criticize, commend, issue instructions, gather data, and simplify complex ideas. We use them to report up the line and to transmit information downward. We even use them to think. Little wonder, then, that the world in general and business in particular prize so highly the ability to communicate.

Yet, probably because everybody has them, anyone with a tongue and a pencil believes he possesses all the prerequisites for effective communication. In a sense, of course, he's right. But, as in most things, it's how effectively you use what you have that makes the difference.

Let us agree, then, that communication is the lifeblood of our workaday world. Get your message across and you will almost certainly do a better job. Conversely, if you communicate in ambiguous or easily misunderstood terms, you will double your work and reduce the caliber of your performance.

Here are some areas where big improvements can be realized with only a little effort.

Talking Your Way to Success

Many people who wouldn't dream of showing up in their offices or places of business unless they were impeccably groomed permit their speech to remain in work clothes. They slur words, choose them poorly, pronounce them incorrectly. They are misunderstood, taken less seriously than they deserve—even ignored sometimes—because their ineffective speech irritates others.

One expert says not to sell the halo effect of good speech short. Most people size others up on very little evidence. If Susan Jones is a neat dresser, those who meet her conclude that she must also be neat about her desk, her paper work, her personal habits, and so on. Similarly, if you speak well, the people who listen to you tend to assume that you possess many other desirable traits.

On reflection, we realize that a man who is neat about his clothes isn't necessarily tidy in his thinking or on his job. But people are often appraised by others through snap judgments. So why not load the dice in your favor in every conceivable way, including better speech?

Fortunately, learning to speak well is like learning any other skill. It begins with determination and a desire to learn. It grows with practice. Eventually, it becomes a self-enforcing habit.

Your Voice

How you *sound* to another individual frequently determines the extent of his attention to, and confidence in, what you are saying. The following suggestions will help you avoid the most common vocal pitfalls.

Bend Your Voice. Your voice is capable of much more than you may think. If you want others to listen to you, make it reflect what you are saying. If you are asking a question, end your sentence with a rising inflection. If you wish to emphasize a part of your thought, speak the key words in your message in a slightly louder voice than the others. At all costs, avoid monotony.

Don't talk like this: ————————————————

Talk like this:

Not Too Fast, Not Too Slow. Any speech habit that calls attention to itself is undesirable. This is especially true of the speed with which you speak, for either extreme detracts noticeably from the content of your message. Talk too fast and your listener may miss an important point. Talk too slowly and he may stifle a yawn and think of other things. What's right? Take your cue from the listener. If he's a fast talker himself, it's probably all right to speak quickly. He's used to it. But if he tends to take his time, take the hint and slow down.

Make It Just Loud Enough. It's a mistake to equate either forcefulness or persuasiveness with loudness. Under the proper circumstances, a whisper can be as dramatic as a shout. If you do your talking in factories, you may have to speak up in order to be heard above the hum of machinery, but ordinarily your listeners will listen more intently if you don't raise your voice to them. Again, you can judge your own performance by observing other people's reactions. If you see them jump or wince, you have two sure signs that your loudness disturbs them. If they lean toward you, tilt their heads, or cup their ears, you know that you need to turn up the volume.

Pitch It Low.   Right or wrong, people tend to react more favorably to a low-pitched voice than to a shrill, high-pitched one. If your own voice lacks body, try the following:

• Relax. Tension tightens and shortens the vocal cords, resulting in a higher pitch.
• Watch your posture. If you speak with your head tilted back or with chin on chest, you strain your throat muscles.
• Use resonance. Sound needs room in order to grow. That's why a cello can produce deeper tones than the smaller violin. You can create the necessary room in your mouth and throat by utilizing your jaws and lips more.

Your Diction

Modulating the tone and rhythm of your speech is not enough. Equally important to your personal success is correct pronunciation. Too many people allow themselves to lapse into lazy speech habits that make their message difficult or even impossible to understand. The man who says, "Blee me" when he means "Believe me," or "Pleny a time," when he means "Plenty of time," is risking not only ineffective communications, but making a poor impression as well.

Frequently, the reason behind bad pronunciation is simple laziness. We allow our lips and tongue to fall into disuse. Consequently, what we say only approximates what we intend to say. Here are some ways to bring clarity to your speech:

Bring Your Lips Together Firmly.   Do you find yourself saying things like "su'scription" and "su'mission" when you mean "subscription" and "submission"? Put your lips together for the *b* sound.

Get the Front of Your Tongue Up. Unless you do, words like *gentle-men, next,* and *world* will come out sounding like, "jemman," "nex'," and "worl'." The *t* and *d* sounds are correctly produced by "exploding" the tip of your tongue against the point where the roof of your mouth meets the back of your teeth. Try it.

Get the Back of Your Tongue Up. Watch out for words like *electric, diagnose,* and *recognize,* for they require that the back of your tongue be up, touching the back of the roof of your mouth. Make a hard *g* sound right now and you'll see what is meant. Get the habit and you will never be guilty of such slovenly diction as "ele'tric," "dia'nose," or "reco'nize."

Watch Your Consonants. Few people neglect to pronounce vowels. Most diction problems center about the rest of the alphabet, the consonants. Give full value to your *m*'s, *n*'s, *ng*'s, *r*'s, and *l*'s in particular.

There isn't a rule or suggestion among those you have just read that need take more than five minutes of your time daily. Considering the payoff in terms of better, more attention-getting speech, you'd have to look a long time to find so modest an investment that yielded such rich dividends.

Say It Clearly

Every employee, whether or not he is in management, necessarily relies on his vocal cords to get much of his day-to-day work done. He gathers information, diagnoses problems, and offers solutions. He conducts business on the telephone, fact to face, and via intercommunication devices. What he says and how he says it frequently mean the difference between getting the job done and chaos. There are several simple methods of ensuring that your oral messages get through.

Use Simple Words. The average individual picks up a number of fancy words without knowing it. For example, he uses *expedite* instead of *speed up, function* instead of *work, utilize* instead of *use.* If you tend to use complicated words, try, in revising your spoken vocabulary, to use the simplest words you can.

Use Easy-to-Hear Words. Certain words don't always register when spoken, for example, *mere, huge,* and *prior*. They're fine in print, even in a letter, but your listener may not hear them clearly, since they are not as familiar as other words that mean the same thing. Steer clear, too, of words that have negative first syllables, like *un-* and *dis-*. The other person may miss that all-important first syllable and understand just the opposite of what you are saying. Suppose, for instance, that you tell him, "A full report is unnecessary." He may *think* he hears, "A full report is necessary." To prevent such a misunderstanding, say, "You don't have to make a full report."

Make One Point at a Time.   Many people habitually crowd a number of thoughts into one sentence. For example: "The new incentive plan should work beautifully because it's easy to set up, takes seniority into consideration, and is geared to pay for itself within five years." When several important ideas are crowded into one sentence, your audience has to be extremely attentive to catch them all. And that's a lot to expect from the average audience. Or individual.

Avoid Generalities.   Certain words are shamelessly overused: *productivity, economy, efficiency,* to name a few. Certainly people know what they mean. But what do they mean in the context of your talk? Suppose you say, "We'll achieve efficiency, economy and many other advantages." Exactly what do you mean by *efficiency* and *economy*? And what are the many advantages? If they are worth mentioning, they are worth naming. Be specific.

Your Vocabulary

The words you use to express your thoughts often tell more than you think. If you frequently grope for the proper expression, if you use words incorrectly, or if you say one thing when you mean another, your listener may feel justified in viewing not only the content of your message but you yourself with some suspicion. However, you can automatically accomplish three important goals if you increase and strengthen your vocabulary.

• You will add precision and clarity to your speech, hence reduce the possibility of being misunderstood.
• You will become a clearer thinker. Since most thinking is verbal, the more words you know, the better equipped you are to juggle ideas.

• You will become persuasive. When you come right down to it, there are just two ways to get things done by others: compulsion and persuasion. Since there are few cases on record of anyone influencing others permanently through brute strength, the only way left is persuasion. And persuasion is 95 percent a matter of words. It's *what you say* that makes people pay attention to you and your ideas.

Here are five tips on how to add power to your own vocabulary.

Learn to Enjoy Words. Every word has its own individual history, or etymology. Make a hobby of words. They can be fun. The sandwich you ate a few hours ago is called that, for example, because it was invented by the earl of Sandwich in 1762, when he spent twenty-four solid hours at the gambling table without taking any food except cold roast beef between slices of toast. We call a despotic ruler a czar because of the man who set the pattern—Caesar. What we refer to as an "apple" started life as a "napple," but the *a* took over the *n*, and what custom joined together, no man has since put asunder. Words big and little (for example, look up *buxom, enthusiasm, malapropism,* and *quidnunc*) have their biographies, and when you get to know them, they become old and familiar friends with whom you associate more easily and admiringly.

Read With a Purpose. As you go through a book or magazine, note the unfamiliar words. Don't just guess at their meanings; look them up and master *all* their meanings. Be aware of what phrases or words hit you particularly and stop to examine why they produce the effect they do. Try saying the same thing in another way and discover for yourself why that combination of words was so effective. This will develop the habit of controlling your own speech.

Listen. To friends. To colleagues and fellow workers. To lectures, discussions, and debates on TV. Jot down those words that are unfamiliar to you and, at the first opportunity, look them up.

Incorporate New Words into Your Speech. Use every new word three times as quickly and naturally as you can, once you have met it. This will make it a part of your vocabulary. And don't be afraid of using unusual words *once* in a while. People will not be insulted by your assumption that they are literate.

Omit Needless Words. Vigorous speech is concise. A sentence should contain no unnecessary words for the same reason that a machine should contain no unnecessary parts. This doesn't mean that you must avoid all detail or make all your sentences short; but every word you utter should *mean* something. Many expressions in common use violate this principle. For example:

Don't Use	Use
the question as to whether	*whether*
owing to the fact that	*because (since)*
with reference to	*about*
in the event that	*if*
for the purpose of	*for*

The Speech

"We'd like to have you address our September meeting."

Drop that simple statement on the average person and the odds are that he or she will do one of three things:

1. Turn it down with some lame excuse.
2. Turn into a pitiful mass of jelly, almost before your eyes.
3. Turn in a performance that, if bottled, could be marketed as an instant tranquilizer.

The sad truth is that most people either dislike making speeches or deliver painfully bad ones. Yet, one of the consequences of being good at what you do is being invited to share your expertise with others from a public platform. As you get better at what you do and your reputation grows, such invitations are apt to multiply.

Of course there is no law that says you must become a speaker. Still, as business and technology grow more complicated, there will be an increasing demand for men and women who can communicate their knowledge to others via the spoken word. And, from a purely selfish viewpoint, people who *can* deliver effective speeches tend to be noticed and remembered.

So there are good and sufficient reasons for sharpening your speech skills. On that assumption, here are some general principles that should help you become a more confident, effective speaker.

Get Your Material Together. Don't confuse an informal or extemporaneous speech with an impromptu performance. An informal performance requires preparation—a great deal, at that; the impromptu job is truly delivered on the spur of the moment. Not one in a hundred people can give more than a passable impromptu speech. Even so consummate a performer as Bob Hope has his best ad libs firmly in mind before he drops them in a monologue or conversation.

The informal speech is not written out word for word but is logically arranged in skeletal form in order to provide you with an orderly plan to follow. The impromptu speech is usually given with little forewarning and is truly ad-libbed.

So the first step is to gather your material. Obviously, you will know a great deal about your subject to begin with; otherwise, you would not have been asked to do the job. But it is seldom possible to prepare a speech *only* from what you know.

Carry a notebook in your pocket. Whenever an idea flashes across your mind, jot it down. When you see something in a newspaper or magazine on your subject, tear it out and add it to your notebook. Since most speaking engagements are arranged well ahead of time, you will find that you have twice as much material as you need fairly early in the game. That's as it should be.

Make an Outline. As you go through your notebook, you will doubtless discover that a lot of the ideas in it are unusable because they are not very good, not very pertinent, or not very original. Eliminate them. What's left after your red penciling will be the raw material of your speech.

Now is the time to arrange that material in some sort of logical sequence. The best way to do this is to draft a skeleton outline of your talk. At this stage, you're better off avoiding complete sentences, because most people can't write the way they talk.

When you write speeches in longhand, your ideas are way ahead of the pencil, and you lose the thread of your thought. You start fishing for words to finish the sentence. The sparkle is gone. Teddy Roosevelt, in preparing speeches, dictated them as rapidly as possible in order to retain a ring of naturalness and spontaneity.

It's true that people in high positions in business and public life prepare their speeches in full manuscript form and read from it. It's an imperative of their station. They can't take any chances on having one wrong word slip out to be misinterpreted or made into political capital. Most speakers, however, do not have to work under this handicap.

Practice delivering the speech as often as necessary to get confidence in your ability. A few practice sessions before a mirror is advisable in order to get an idea of how you look and which gestures are most effective. Add a tape recorder and you can hear how you sound as well.

Your Opening. With the rough outline done, you are ready to work on the opening. For a very good reason, this is the one portion of your speech that should be written out in advance; you should know exactly how and where to start your remarks when you get up in front of your audience. Because your opening will determine whether or not you hold your audience's attention, make it a "grabber"—something so intrinsically interesting that your listeners will be compelled to listen.

Begin With an Anecdote. It can be humorous, built around a famous person, or connected to a famous event. It should be germane to your subject, but fascinating in itself.

Start By Throwing Down a Challenge. A challenge seldom goes unanswered. It's as old as knighthood and as modern as a boy with a chip on his shoulder. How do you do it? The surest way is to make it personal. Talk about an interest your audience must possess: safety, success, security, decreased costs, increased profits, and so on, then phrase it in such a way as to dare them, question them, defy them, or invite them to a contest. For example, you might say, "Not one person in this room is doing his job as well as he might," or "When was the last time you had a good idea?" or, "Suppose you were fired tomorrow."

Dramatize Your Idea. "Without this little earthworm I hold in my hand, man would disappear from the earth. Sound ridiculous? It's true. This little blind, insignificant wriggler is the most important of all living animals. Why? Because without him, the vegetable world would vanish. And then the animal world would disappear and the human race would perish."

That was the beginning of a few words about earthworms, on the surface the least promising subject for drama. Yet it galvanized the audience's attention and was the opening of a very successful talk.

The founder of Methodism, John Wesley, once faced a congregation on a warm day in which some people were falling asleep. He suddenly shouted, "Fire! Fire!" The congregation, startled out of its lethargy, cried "Where? Where?" Wesley's reply: "In Hell—for people who sleep in church!" Everyone stayed awake from that moment on.

There isn't a subject in the world that can't be dramatized, so don't beg off with, "I can't talk that way." What you are really saying is that you haven't bothered to dramatize events, to relate fragments of conversations, to create suspense, to build to a climax, to enact different characters. Yet these are the very things that create interest. In short, you dramatize ideas by painting word pictures.

Your Closing. Now forget the body of your talk temporarily and plan your closing. At this stage, it is always well to summarize briefly the points covered, repeating each for emphasis. Then apply the same principle as for the opening: Write out the last sentence so that when it comes time to finish, you have a definite doorway through which to exit. We've all heard speakers who hit the climax only to ruin it by getting their second wind and continuing. This usually happens when the speaker doesn't definitely know in advance what "handle" he is going to use for bringing his talk to a close. After you have delivered your closing sentence, give your audience a nod, smile, and sit down. It is no discourtesy to omit thanking your audience. In fact, a "thank you" weakens your talk by seeming to apologize to an audience that should be appreciative of the message you have given them.

When You're on Your Feet. Let's say you have accepted an invitation to speak on human relations in industry before a group of business and professional people. The man who invited you to speak is president of a manufacturing company with one hundred employees. You feel confident that you will have his attention immediately because every day he has many problems pertaining to human relations in his industry. But in addition to him, the audience will consist of bankers, lawyers, doctors, and retailers. What kind of opening can you use to get everyone's attention?

The first step is to pause a few seconds after being introduced. With a pleasant expression, glance around at your audience and give each individual a chance to settle down and refocus his attention on you. If some people haven't stopped their private conversations, nothing will get them to clam up more surely than your remaining quiet for a few seconds. These few seconds of pause will also inspire confidence in you on the part of the audience because it is a mark of an experienced speaker.

After you get into position, look out over the audience. Survey it as a whole, then look directly at some individual. If you spot someone with a genial countenance, give him a smile whether or not you are acquainted with him. The entire audience will establish contact with you mentally as a result of your demonstration of interest. You are now ready for the opening.

Keep it casual. Turn to the person who introduced you and say, "Thank You, Mr. Rogers." Then turn to your audience with a leisurely, "Good evening, ladies and gentlemen" or "Good evening, members of the XYZ group." Then comes your opening.

Start with your "grabber." Quickly show how it relates to them. For instance: "Good human relations can be worth a thousand dollars or more annually to each person here this evening. Even though you may not be an employer yourself, you have a vital stake in industrial peace. And there are specific ways in which you can help maintain it."

With these opening remarks you have built a bridge from your "grabber" to the attention of the audience. Then dive into the main body of your talk. Develop the points you want to make and be sure to make them in terms of the interests of your listeners.

Now you are ready for your close. It may be so simple and positive a statement as, "You people of Middletown know the value of good industrial relations to this community. You've proved that by your presence here this evening. By supporting the kind of program I have described, you can help improve them." Then you nod to your audience, smile, turn, and walk back to your chair. Remember, no "thank you."

Miscellaneous Tips. To gain poise and add liveliness to your talk, follow these suggestions:

Talk Unhurriedly. You should have time to take good, solid breaths. Otherwise, you risk voice failure, a condition in which your voice becomes shaky, breathless, and weak.

Don't Memorize Your Speech. You will only create an additional fear: that of forgetting something. Besides, memorized words tend to take on a singsong quality.

Pause Occasionally. This enables you to collect your thoughts; it allows what you have said to sink in, and it works to good dramatic effect.

Do the Unexpected. Is the audience's attention wandering? You can recapture it by suddenly pointing to something. You can walk across the stage or up an aisle. You can pour yourself a glass of water and drink it calmly. You can tear up your notes (providing you don't need them). You can toss a coin in the air, drop a book to the floor, ring a bell, clap your hands. Startle your audience to attention.

Don't Be Thrown by Nervousness. Senator William Borah of Idaho once said, "I don't think any speaker is fit to face an audience unless he feels a quickening of the pulse." Every speaker needs nervous energy to put his message across effectively. To stabilize that energy, however, take a couple of deep breaths before you get up to speak. Then let yourself go, putting your entire body behind your message, using gestures to emphasize your points. After the first few sentences, as you warm up to your subject, you'll forget the butterflies.

Writing With Impact

Many of the techniques of effective speaking can be applied to your written messages, whether they are letters, reports, or memos. For whether your audience is hearing you through its ears of eyes, it will respond equally strongly to the same devices: simple words, one idea at a time, specifics rather than generalities, a precise (not ostentatious) vocabulary, a "grabber" opening, and so on.

But in addition, by the nature of its visual quality, the written word offers other opportunities for clarity and impact. If you suspect that your letters are a bit dull or pedestrian, here are seven ways to inject life into them:

1. State your purpose right off the bat. The opening paragraph, and usually the opening sentence, should tell the reader your purpose. Letters that begin with, "You'll be glad to learn" or "I thought you'd like to know" attract immediate attention.

2. For emphasis, try a question-and-answer instead of a flat statement: "How long should this take? Less than one hour."

3. Occasionally prod your reader with a one- or two-word paragraph: "Yessir." "It worked!" "Think again."

4. Use asterisks or numerals to separate parts of a series: There are three reasons why this is a good idea:
   *It's inexpensive.

*It requires no extra personnel.

*It saves time.

5. To drive home a point, use a quotation and name its author: "As Dr. Johnson said, 'There is no problem devised by man that cannot also be solved by man.'" But be careful. This is an easy device to overuse.

6. If you wish to emphasize something in a letter, add it in ink as a postscript beneath the main, typewritten portion of the letter. It needn't be an afterthought; it can be built solidly into the letter's strategy.

7. Use the recipient's name once, but no more, in the body of the letter, wherever you want him to read with extra attention: "Despite the immediate cost, Mr. Carter, the plan looks good to us because . . ." If you use his name more than once, though, you will give your letter an unpleasant apple-polishing tone.

Ten Commandments for Writing
Better Business Letters

To many of the people with whom you deal, your letters are you. They've never seen you. They've never shaken your hand. They may never even have spoken to you. The only way they have of sizing you up is through the words you put on paper. The right words, correctly strung together, sell you. The wrong words have the opposite effect. There are ten cardinal rules for turning out letters that do their job.

Be Clear. We can forgive a business letter much if its meaning is clear. Say what you mean. Use short words. Reread what you've written through the other fellow's eyes. If *you* received your letter, would you understand it?

Be Correct. Get your facts right, as well as your form. Check your vocabulary, spelling, grammar, punctuation.

Be Complete. It's better to give more than has been requested than too little. It can save time. It can eliminate misunderstandings. It may save additional costly correspondence.

Be Concise. This is no contradiction of the rule Be Complete. A letter can be both complete and concise, for being concise means saying everything necessary in as few words as possible. Study the headlines in any newspaper for a quick understanding of this commandment. You'll see precious few adjectives, adverbs, or modifying clauses.

Be Courteous. Regardless of how you feel toward your correspondent, it always pays to be courteous, if only because it's impossible to retract a thought once it has been committed to paper. If you are polite, should you ever have to eat your words, they'll at least be sweet to the taste.

Be Considerate. This is more than merely being courteous; it means putting yourself in the recipient's place and writing the kind of letter you'd like to get if conditions were reversed. With some thought, even a dressing down in a letter can be made palatable. It will most likely be more effective too.

Be Conversational. Write to your reader as if you had just met him in person and were speaking to him informally. That means avoiding jargon, using contractions, resorting occasionally to a colloquialism, sticking to the active voice. There is no such thing as a special language of business correspondence other than the language of everyday conversation.

Be Cheerful. No one likes to read bad news. So, whatever the burden of your message, give it graciously and cheerfully.

Be Confident. You should be certain of the validity of the information you are giving, of your ability to handle whatever results from your business letter, of the recipient's doing what you are asking him or her to. Confidence in yourself breeds confidence in you by others.

Be Clever. There's nothing in the books that says you can't be human or humorous or clever. There is little enough wit in the world as it is. So share yours.

The Memo

When overused, memos can merely add to your paperwork. But used properly, they can be powerful communication tools that save you time and energy. They can establish goals, pinpoint deadlines, set responsibilities, eliminate misunderstandings, and reduce the number of time-devouring meetings you attend. But how much help you get from your memos depends on how good they are. They needn't be literary gems, but they should be clear and to the point. Some questions to ask yourself:

• Why is it being written? Are you seeking information? Offering clarification? Attempting to persuade? Unless you know where you're going, the memo will ramble and lack force.
• Is it self-contained? Is all pertinent background material cited or explained? Or will the recipient have to call you for additional data? If it's necessary for your reader to know that you are referring to statistics drawn up by the Department of Commerce in the August bulletin, mention that fact. Unless it can stand by itself, a memo is less than completely effective.
• Will the recipient learn something from it? If he won't, why should he read it? Your job is to make sure he learns something from your memo— your recommendation, new facts, late developments, whatever.
• What's in it for you? Will it save you time? Eliminate the need to deal with middlemen? Settle an issue? Put you on record as favoring or disapproving some course of action? Unless you benefit from it in some way, it may not be worth your while.

The Report

The primary function of a report is to inform the reader clearly, concisely, and accurately of the results of some research or analysis. To do this properly, the report should set forth all information relevant to the purpose and scope of the job and omit all irrelevant information.

Next the report should be so constructed that the reader understands the results of the work that preceded it. This means that the facts must be presented in proper sequence and detailed to whatever extent called for by the character of the subject and the requirements of the reader. To do this properly requires close attention to planning the organization of the report.

Some people have enough talent or experience to draw up a good plan of organization with little difficulty. But most can profit from a somewhat more formalized method. The following procedure, although it may seem oversimplified, will help you produce a well-planned, cohesive, understandable report.

A word of warning: There are two bad habits report writers seem to get into even when they recognize the need for planning: deciding upon a framework for the report *before* reviewing the material to fit within that framework; and selecting an organizational pattern from some similar previous report and attempting to adapt it to the present job. Either of these practices results in a contrived pattern. The subject matter of each particular job and the available material should determine the framework to be used.

Start by writing a brief one-sentence statement for yourself that sets forth the purpose and scope of your report. By keeping this statement always at hand, you will be constantly reminded of your objectives as you assemble your material and prepare your report. Next, review all notes, excerpts, and other data that you have gathered during the study, jotting down on small cards each major or minor subject dealt with by this material. Then check these cards against your one-sentence statement of intent with a view to eliminating any irrelevant material and determining where more material may be needed.

Next sort the cards by subject into main groupings. That way you will spot any duplication of material as well as the principal divisions of your final organizational pattern.

You must now decide how to arrange those principal divisions. The sequence may be deductive, where one subject leads to another, or the various subjects may be presented without relationship to one another but all leading to one conclusion. The final arrangement will depend on the character of the material.

Before adopting any arrangement as final, consider whether the pattern you have chosen will be the most effective in achieving the desired objective, for it is unlikely that there will be more than one best arrangement. Once you decide on a framework, the writing of the report should be carried out in strict accordance with this outline.

Some report writers feel that most of the time spent on planning is wasted. But concern with planning usually results in a gain rather than a loss, for if errors in approach can be discovered while the framework is being developed, the time and expense devoted to revising the more hastily written report can be avoided. The finished job will be better and more useful to the reader for whom it is intended.

The Meeting

There is a great deal of talk about the importance of good communications between a manager and his people, but relatively little about how to go about realizing this worthy goal.

Chat with your people on an informal basis, by all means. Let them know they can visit you almost at will, certainly. Encourage them to ask questions, verbalize their gripes, voice their convictions—absolutely.

And yet, important as these casual avenues of intercourse may be, they cannot replace the formally structured meeting as an efficient vehicle for gathering and transmitting information. Properly conducted, the meeting is an unbeatable way to zero in on a problem, discuss strategies, weigh alternatives, and reach a consensus. As a manager, you are occasionally compelled to hold meetings, and whether they fly or flop largely depends on your skill.

Despite the formal atmosphere generated by a group of people gathered around a table or in an auditorium, you will largely defeat your purpose if you make your meeting too stiff. Any appearance of formality will be picked up by the group, and the result will be a stuffy session—precisely what you want to avoid. An easy, natural manner on your part will transmit itself to the group and encourage its members to relax and speak freely.

At the same time, it's important to start your meetings on time. If you make it your business to begin promptly, your people will make it theirs to be punctual.

Put your people at ease. A simple opening such as "Shall we get started?" delivered in a conversational tone is very effective. Make a few opening, nonbusiness remarks to break the ice and set a friendly tone. If anyone is a stranger to the group, make sure he or she is introduced.

When the group is at ease, point out that as the leader, your chief role will be to raise questions and problems and to keep the discussion on target; it is not to act as an expert. Invite each person to participate and be sure everyone has an opportunity to talk.

Present the Problem. "A problem well stated is half solved." It's true. And as the leader of the meeting you must phrase your problem or subject so that it is easily understood by the group.

It helps to state the problem on a chart or blackboard so that your people can keep it firmly in mind as the discussion progresses. Then show them why it is important, tell them something of its background (when the problem was first noted and under what circumstances, for example) and cite a specific case or illustration to clarify the subject. If necessary, define any technical jargon likely to be used in the course of the meeting.

Tell your people the purpose of the meeting in such a way that they know what you are seeking from them (for example, "What I'm looking for are workable suggestions to prevent another such loss to the competition"). Finally, outline the procedure to be followed.

Get the Discussion Rolling.   Self-evident though it may be, you ought to make certain that everyone understands the problem before launching your discussion. The easiest way is to ask them. "Is the problem clear to everyone?" "Will you help us, Pete, by spelling out the parameters of this department's authority?" "Can anyone offer a specific example of the breakdown in communications?"—such questions can dissolve uncertainties and help everybody comprehend what's at stake.

Once everyone understands the problem, you are ready to enter into a discussion. But people are frequently reluctant to begin talking. Here's where you, as moderator, come in with some opening statements to get the ball rolling:

"We've all had some experience with this. What particular experiences apply here?"

"I could put a number of things up on the board under this objective. What particular considerations would you say are most important? I'll jot them down as you tick them off."

"I've roughly outlined the reasons why this problem is important to us, and we've taken a look at our objectives. Let's begin with objective one. Who has something important we can place under this objective?"

Conduct the Discussion.   This is where the meeting really starts. And if it is to be fruitful, you must encourage discussion through well-planned questions that the group can understand without fear of embarrassment or ignorance. To accomplish this, create a free, permissive climate that encourages participation by everyone. That means making sure that each person takes an active part in the meeting while you fade into the background.

In order to shift most of the load to the participants, use thought-provoking questions to get viewpoints, then make a statement or throw out another question based on the opinion. This will keep the discussion moving along, because no two people think precisely alike.

When one phase of the discussion, or a particular aspect of the problem, has been brought to a conclusion, you should provide a transition of some sort to the next topic, showing how it naturally follows from what has preceded.

Generally, it is your responsibility to keep the discussion on track by restating the objective from time to time, postponing side issues until the main issue is decided and identifying irrelevant remarks. A well-planned meeting has definite, concrete objectives, and, as leader, you must see that the available time is appropriately used, not frittered away.

To keep the discussion on the beam, you might inject such observations as: "Are we going off on a tangent? Let's get back to the question that Jane raised a moment ago." "Would you mind holding that question for a few minutes when we'll have a chance to consider it more thoroughly?" "Is that pertinent to the objective that we agreed belongs on the board?"

Virtually every meeting hits a dead spot at one point or another. Everyone clams up. There seem to be no more ideas left anywhere. It may very well be that you have exhausted one particular vein and it's time to move on to another. Or you may be barking up the wrong tree. Again, it's up to you to act as a catalytic agent and keep things moving.

You might summarize what you've covered so far. Or ask your people if they feel that the point has been fully covered. Or invite questions, additions, or criticisms of what you have put on the blackboard.

Finally, you should try to get commitment from the group. For after all points have been discussed, weighed, and evaluated, there comes a time when the participants must decide what's to be *done*.

To help things along, you might emphasize the importance of action at this point by summarizing the group's conclusions, thus crystallizing its thinking for each member, then asking the participants if they reaffirm those conclusions. If they do, this is the time to invite action: "From the work done so far, we've come to a definite decision as to what should be done. Now the question is, how do we get the ball rolling?" What follows should be an agreed-upon plan of action to effect the group's conclusion.

Finishing Up. Ideally, participants should leave your meeting with the feeling that something substantial has been accomplished; conclusions should be clear and definite. As leader, you should summarize the highlights of the discussion and emphasize the major conclusions that have been reached.

In your summary, make sure that the group knows what it is expected to do or what it has decided to do as a result of the meeting.

If there is to be another meeting (to receive further recommendations from a committee, for example), announce the time and place as well as why it is necessary.

Congratulate the group on its work during the meeting and wish the participants good luck in carrying out their decisions.

Finally, conclude the meeting as naturally as it was started with a simple statement such as, "That completes our session for today. I'll look forward to seeing you next week."

If possible, remain a few minutes after the meeting if anyone seems anxious to talk with you. But be careful not to keep him talking too long. He may have other duties or commitments and not know how to break away.

While events are fresh in your mind, now is the time to hold a post-mortem of your meeting. If it ran overtime, for instance, you may have tried to cover too much ground or been too permissive and allowed it to wander or spent too much time on minor points. Next time try to do better.

Here are some specific questions that you should ask yourself after each meeting. They may reveal to you one or more particular areas of weakness. Concentrate upon them in your next meeting and you'll notice a marked improvement.

How clear were the group's goals?

How were the goals determined? By whom?

How did the group make decisions?

How effective and permanent are the decisions?

How well did the group work at its task? Did it loaf or make good progress?

To what extent was the discussion "up in the clouds"? What was the group atmosphere? Warm and friendly? Threatening and hostile?

To what extent did members seem to have private thoughts, unarticulated feelings, or opinions that they weren't comfortable enough to bring out into the open?

To what extent were the minority views listened to with respect?

When confronted with differences in feelings and ideas, what did the group do?

Which two members can most easily influence others to change their opinions?

Which two are least able to influence others?

Which two tend to withdraw from active discussion when strong differences begin to appear?

Which two wanted the group to be friendly and comfortable?

Which two tried to do the most to keep the group on the ball?

Did you try to do too much, ending up dominating instead of overseeing?

There are many persuasive reasons for holding meetings. A good meeting can help you get to know your people better because it gives you a chance to observe each of them in a problem-solving environment. At the same time, it should help you wrestle successfully with your tougher problems. And not to be overlooked is the *esprit de corps* created by providing your people with a common goal.

So work at making your meetings successful. They can help you become a more effective manager.

Clearly, the ability to communicate is a bedrock-basic requisite for success in business, for virtually everything you do on your job, from asking questions to criticizing someone else's idea, depends on it. Performance, morale, and cooperation are largely based on understanding, and understanding, in turn, depends on good communications.

You cannot hope to be an effective manager if you have difficulty in clarifying the nature of an assignment or a problem that your department is facing. Clear communication, in short, helps get things done expeditiously by reducing or eliminating altogether the possibility of misunderstanding or error. And managers who consistently get things done make themselves likely candidates for promotion.

Because the ability to communicate is so fundamental a skill, we will now consider two special aspects of it: how to share your knowledge with others and how to sell your ideas. In the next two chapters, then, we turn to the art of teaching and the tested techniques of persuasion.

9

How to Teach

To one degree or another, we are all teachers.

The businessperson issues instructions to suppliers, information to customers, directions to employees.

The professional simplifies his specialized skills and knowledge in order to make them intelligible to the laymen he serves.

The salesperson demonstrates his products to prospects; explains why his line is superior to his competitor's; details his firm's delivery schedules, credit policies, promotional plans, and trade-in allowances.

The manager? He is continually imparting knowledge to the people in his department, motivating them, explaining new methods and rules, overseeing and judging their performance. He passes along and interprets company policy, answers questions, and helps solve problems. Teaching is one of his most important functions.

Good Teaching Isn't Difficult

Since teaching is so large a part of your job, it follows that the more proficient you become at it, the more effective a manager you will be. Your main function, after all, is to get things done through people. Adding to their skills, knowledge, and self-confidence—in short, teaching them—is one major way of accomplishing that. Fortunately, it is easier to be a good teacher than a bad one, for teaching is a logical process, with a distinct beginning, middle, and end. Many of its techniques are based on common sense. And it is efficient. Here are the simple rules that work.

Know Your Material

Too often those whose job it is to impart information to others assume that because they have been on the job longer than their students and therefore know a few facts that their students do not, they can ad-lib their way through any teaching session.

Not so.

The more you know about a subject, the easier it is to explain it to others. Under such circumstances, your words flow smoothly, intelligibly. You are in a position to anticipate, and answer, questions. Your mind is a treasure trove of facts, pertinent examples, and illustrations.

When you try to get by with a smattering of knowledge, you will fall into all kinds of traps. Sooner or later you will confront the clever subordinate who will test your knowledge with a tricky question and quickly expose you. You will run into the employee who does not catch on quickly and asks for another example, and again you will give yourself away. You will unwittingly pass on misinformation. Most important of all, you will not teach anyone anything.

The cardinal rule of all good teaching, therefore, is: Know your material.

Know What You Want to Get Across. Just what do you want your student to learn? How to fill out an expense account? How your company's insurance plan works? The proper procedure for requisitioning equipment? Before you can reasonably expect him to grasp your instructions, you must have them clear in your own mind. If necessary, write them out so that you can refer to them.

Know the Latest Facts. If you are still citing old company rules and policies to an employee after they have been changed, you are setting the stage for misunderstanding and ill will. The rule: Keep your knowledge up-to-date.

Admit Ignorance. Honesty is a supreme virtue in teaching. If you do not know the answer to a question or the solution to a problem, don't try to double-talk your way out of it. Nobody expects you to be infallible. What every one of your people does have a right to expect from you is a frank admission that you do not know and a promise to find out the answer and report it promptly. What you should know, therefore, is whom you can call upon within your own company for further information (for example, personnel, accounting, shipping), what manuals or other documents exist on the subject, what outside sources are at your disposal.

Organize Your Presentation

Knowledge of your material alone is no guarantee of adequate preparation. You must be able to transmit what you know to others in a lucid, intelligible manner. This requires organization—a logical, coherent arrangement of the various facts you want to get across.

What you are teaching will usually dictate your method of organization. If, for example, you are showing an employee how to operate a machine, you will probably organize your instructions in a chronological sequence ("First you do this; second, you do that; third, you do this.") If you are explaining why certain modifications are being made in a product, you might organize your presentation along the lines of cause and effect ("The line had to be priced high because of the metal parts we used. Some customers objected to this. The result was less demand for it. Consequently, we had to increase our prices. With the new plastic elements, we'll be able to reduce prices. Therefore . . .")

The important thing is to impose some kind of logic, some system, on your material so that, in the presentation, one point leads naturally and smoothly to another.

Have All Necessary Tools On Hand

"It's easy. You simply use a Form 490. . . . Where's that form? Wait a minute. Oh, yes. Here it is. You take Form 490 and—*this* isn't Form 490! Perkins, will you run over to Overmyer's office and ask her to give us a Form 490. Thanks. While we're waiting for Perkins, I'd llke to emphasize how important it is to keep copies of everything you requisition on a Form 490. . . ."

About as interesting as last month's newspaper, isn't it? The workers attending that imaginary session can't help but conclude that Form 490 isn't really very important. Even worse, while they're waiting for Perkins to return, they'll lose the gist of what their manager was saying. They'll forget what preceeded that awkward interruption. They'll daydream. The delicate thread of their attention will be badly frayed, if not severed.

Many managers who give instructions in the course of their work overlook the importance of having their props in good working order and available in advance. Yet, such tools add interest to what they are saying; they help underscore certain points and turn vague ideas into concrete reality.

If you need special equipment to demonstrate or explain your lesson, make sure it is where it ought to be and that it is in good working order. If you will be using a rubber band, make sure it isn't broken. If you will need chalk, have several pieces. If you will be switching on a motor, make sure it is working properly beforehand. If you plan on using a movie projector, check the film in advance and have it ready to roll.

Be Enthusiastic

One of your chief duties is to stimulate your people. If you show by voice or manner that you find what you are saying dull and uninteresting, the person you are trying to teach will catch the virus of boredom from you. He, too, will find the material dull and, consequently, either not learn it or learn it poorly.

So a basic element of preparing yourself to teach anything is to whip up some old-fashioned enthusiasm for the subject. Usually, when you know a subject well, you are naturally enthusiastic over it. But should you find your enthusiasm for it waning, here are three quick ways to build a bonfire under your flagging interest:

• Act enthusiastic even if you have to act, for enthusiasm creates its own momentum. Feign it for a while, and it will become genuine.
• Review the advantages of getting your lesson across. Will you get better performances from your people? Increase your department's efficiency? Derive satisfaction of some kind? As a result of your successful teaching, you will reap some benefit. Identify it and watch your enthusiasm grow!
• Put yourself in your student's shoes. He's depending on you for information: an explanation, illumination, or help of some kind. Why not give him a break and present it in as exciting a manner as possible?

Once you are prepared—that is, you know your material, have it organized, have all the necessary tools, and are enthusiastic—you are ready for the next major step.

Be Sensitive

Getting information across isn't a one-way street. If it were, there wouldn't be such a crying need for effective managers. Printed instruction sheets would do their informational job for them.

No. Effective teaching is based on the interplay of two or more human beings. There is give and take, questions and answers, action and reaction. A teacher can see whether or not his message is getting across and backtrack, simplify, explain, illustrate, and elaborate accordingly. Books, tape recordings, or movies, helpful though they may be as teaching aids, can never replace live teachers, particularly if the teacher knows how to make his subject both interesting and clear.

Here's what it takes to get your knowledge across.

Present the Big Picture

Since learning is more effective when a person understands where the information is leading him, you can dramatically increase comprehension by offering your student a bird's-eye view of the material you will be covering before you actually begin your lesson.

If you are instructing a group of people, you might pass out a one-page outline of what you will be covering. If you are speaking to an individual, you might synopsize in an informal way what you are about to tell him. (For example, "I'm going to show you how to fill out your performance plan for next year and evaluate the relative importance of your major responsibilities.") The important thing is to help your audience see and understand, with one sweeping view, where you—and they—are going. In doing so, you not only prove that the trip is worthwhile, you also make it easier for them to accompany you.

When you can, therefore, sketch the big picture for your people before filling in the details.

Break the Material Down into Digestible Parts

Once you have outlined your material for your student, dissect it for him. Lead him by the hand, so to speak, through the various parts that constitute the whole. This approach offers two advantages. It gives the student a chance to absorb gradually what you are teaching (such learning "sticks" far better than knowledge that is crammed). And it enables you to pinpoint those areas that are not perfectly clear and that are giving him trouble.

One vital point; Your job is to break your material down in order to make it more easily comprehended. This means that each unit must be an entity in itself; each individual part must make sense to your student.

For example, if you are attempting to explain your company's new tuition-refund program to an employee, you might divide the subject into *(a)* past educational refund policies; *(b)* shortcomings of the old program; *(c)* the new tuition-refund program; and *(d)* why the new program is an improvement over the old.

You would *not* break it down, say, into *(a)* how the new program differs from the old; *(b)* possible shortcomings of the new program; *(c)* educational experiences of other employees; and *(d)* your personal philosophy of education. Such a breakdown would be confusing and difficult to comprehend.

Keep your parts understandable.

Maintain a Logical Sequence

Since learning is based largely on memory, your success as a teacher depends on your ability to present your material in the most memorable fashion possible. A logical arrangement helps you do just that; by establishing correlations and relationships between points, it adds meaning to them. And what makes sense is most easily remembered.

Start at the Beginning. Many managers discourage their people from learning by plunging too deeply and too suddenly into their material. They omit a vital first step or basic idea either because it is *so* basic (to them!) or because they have neglected to identify it in the first place. If you really want to get your knowledge across, ask yourself, "What is the actual beginning of my lesson?" before you open your mouth. Then start with that!

Move from the Simple to the Complex. By starting with what is easy, then moving on to the more difficult, you not only make your lesson simpler to grasp, you give your student all-important confidence in his or her ability to master the subject.

Explain Why. "You must always depress the pedal before extracting the mold because it opens this clamp. If you don't step on the pedal, the mold will shatter when you remove it." "Be sure to keep the pink copy of your expense-account sheet, just in case Accounting has any questions." "Take two salt pills during the heat cycle. They'll prevent heat exhaustion due to excessive perspiration." Give reasons why what you are saying is so; show the connection between the facts or ideas and your student will remember what you have told him—because he understands it.

Demonstrate

"Words fail me."

We've all used that expression at one time or another, and sometimes it's true. Occasionally, words aren't enough to clarify a thought. When they aren't, it's time to use action. By doing something or showing something to your student, you can frequently make clear in an instant what might otherwise require many minutes, even hours, of talking. It is, for example, a great deal easier to demonstrate how to ride a bicycle than to verbalize it.

A demonstration packs a greater wallop than words, too, because it immediately translates an abstract concept into a visual reality. A good salesman, for example, won't tell you, "These trousers are wrinkle resistant," and leave it at that. He will deliberately and ceremoniously tie a knot in one pants leg, tighten it with a grunt, then untie it for your inspection.

The plain fact is that everybody likes a show. We are attracted by and pay attention to movement, action, things happening. We put more credence in our eyes than in our ears. And we appreciate the change of pace from words, words, words to action. Whenever possible, therefore, demonstrate and dramatize your lesson. Draw a picture. Hand your student a chart for his inspection. Show him a photograph, a blueprint, a scale model. Write something on a blackboard. Hit a safety-glass lens with a hammer. Point to a piece of equipment. Invite him to throw a switch. Flip a coin. Ring a bell. Shoot off a firecracker. Stand on your head if it will drive home the point.

Do something! Something that will help clarify what you have just said, emphasize what you are saying, or call attention to what you are about to say.

Accentuate the Positive

The human brain is a delicate—and sometimes ornery—mechanism. It doesn't always listen the way we'd like it to. And it is far from infallible.

Tell it *not* to do something, and in the process of transmitting the pro-
hibition to the rest of your body, it may activate the very muscles that
ought to be relaxed.

Anyone who has ever used a typewriter is familiar with this kind of
mental short circuit. Type a word incorrectly, and as you are erasing it,
you will think, "I mustn't repeat that error." No sooner do your fingers
begin to move again than—lo and behold!—you repeat the error in five
cases out of ten.

Thus, if you say, "Betty, don't throw the lever if the light goes out,"
it's even money that Betty's brain will erroneously associate throwing the
lever with the extinguished light. She'll pull a blank on the restriction. It
is far more effective to say, "Betty, throw the lever only when the light
flashes on."

So, if you want to avoid errors and misunderstandings, keep your
instructions positive.

Repeat, Repeat, Repeat

There is an old teaching axiom that goes: "First, tell 'em what you're
going to tell 'em; then tell 'em; then tell 'em what you've told 'em." It's
sound advice because sheer repetition hammers information into the
brain, a fact of life that advertisers have been cashing in on for some time.

This doesn't mean that you should tell an employee, "Turn this key to
start the machine, turn this key to start the machine, turn this key to
start the machine." He will not only think that you consider him an
idiot; he will have his suspicions about you too.

No. The kind of repetition required is far more subtle. It consists of
saying substantially the same thing at *spaced intervals in different ways.*
If you instruct your student, "Turn this key to start the machine," for
example, you might go on to describe the next several steps, obliquely
return to the subject by observing, "Just as you started the machine by
turning the key, you activate the cutting blade by turning this knob,"
continue with other matters, and wind up with, "As easy as it was to
start the machine by turning the key, that's how simple it is to stop it—
you just turn the key back."

Not every point you make will require repetition. But no matter what
material you are dealing with, there will be certain main points that you
wish to drive home. Know which these are before you face your student
and prepare well in advance the various forms your repetition will take.

Provide Practice

What we do reinforces learning because it impresses not only our eyes and ears but also establishes a motor habit—a certain pattern of behavior. By learning with our muscles, we are really repeating to ourselves in an additional language the verbal lesson to which we have just been exposed. And repetition, we have seen, is one valid avenue of learning.

In your teaching, therefore, provide opportunities for the student to practice whenever possible. If you have been explaining how to pack a crate, let him take a crack at packing one himself. If you want him to master a new safety procedure, give him a chance to go through its steps.

Practice may not *always* make perfect, but it sure helps.

Make Sure It Sticks

One of the chief purposes of teaching is to alter the thinking or behavior of an individual or group somehow. It follows that you, the teacher, should take positive steps to ensure that your material makes not only an immediate impression but a lasting one as well. You want your lesson to stick with your student long after you have finished talking.

As you wind up your presentation, therefore, use the following techniques.

Review. Assuming that what you have been teaching is reasonably complex in nature, you owe it to your students to "tell 'em what you've told 'em." This should be a succinct recapitulation of the most important points covered during the teaching session.

It may take as little as a minute, as long as five, but seldom much more. Just as you gave the big picture before actually diving into the details, now it becomes your job to present another sweeping view of your subject from the vantage point of hindsight.

This is the time to emphasize basic principles and fundamental ideas and to skip specifics. Some teachers like to jot down key words around which they may elaborate. Others prefer to write out an actual half-page synopsis beforehand in order to avoid omitting anything important. Whatever method you employ, use the review principle. It helps make knowledge stick.

Encourage Questions. It's a rare teacher, and a rarer student, who plays his or her role to perfection. Despite all your preparations and precautions, you will almost always bat a little less than 1.000. An ambiguous word, a not quite pertinent example, a too-rapid pace—something is bound to sabotage your lesson somewhere along the line. And despite his or her best intentions, your student will probably tune you out for several seconds at a time (long enough to miss a vital point or two).

So encourage questions by asking, "Have I failed to make anything clear?"; by not showing irritation no matter how foolish a question may be; by doing your very best to answer every single one asked.

Quiz Them. Some students are bashful. Some feel that asking a question diminishes them in some way. Others just want to get the lesson over with as quickly and painlessly as possible.

If, after encouragement, few, if any, questions are forthcoming, take the initiative and ask some pointed questions yourself. "What's the recommended way to lift a heavy load?" "Leslie, what would you do if the computer suddenly went down in the middle of a run?" "Who should see copies of all memos going out from this department?" Questions like these will pinpoint misunderstandings and nip errors in the bud.

Be pleasant, but be a bit relentless too. The two are not incompatible.

Pat Them on the Back. The sweetest music of all: praise!

Everybody likes to hear a "Well done!" so don't be miserly with your approval or admiration. If your student performs a new job well, tell him so. If he answers a difficult question easily, let him know it. If he asks a relevant, provocative question, congratulate him on it. By doing so, you will encourage him to live up to a high standard of achievement, motivate him to continue to learn, and increase his confidence in his abilities.

Finally, then, leave him with a pat on the back. He'll not only be a better student—and more effective employee—for it; he'll be convinced that you are a remarkably discerning teacher!

You will certainly be a more effective manager.

10

How to Sell Your Ideas

Ideas have always been a priceless ingredient of business success. Today they are in greater demand than ever before. Caught between rising costs, on the one hand, and keener competition, on the other, industry has, in self-defense, put itself on a continuous alert for ways to boost efficiency, cut expenses, and improve market share. There is a ceaseless search for new, profitable technologies, products, methods, and materials.

These precious ideas come from just one source—people. People like you.

But having an idea, even a brilliant one, is only half the equation. You must also breathe life into it by expressing it persuasively in order to get others to adopt it.

That's the real need. To a great extent your success in landing the big jobs ahead hinges on how well you answer the ever-present demand for people who not only can think but can also sell their ideas.

We're All Salespeople

The truth is, we are all in the business of selling.

Consider, for example, what you really did when you proposed to your wife. Didn't you promise to do everything in your power to make her happy? Didn't you take special pains to package your product (you!) as attractively as possible? Didn't you try to outdeserve the competition?

Remember how you got your first job? Again the product was you and the odds are that you "sold" yourself by emphasizing the benefits your future employer would realize if he "bought" what you were selling—a competent, willing worker, reliable, trustworthy, and skilled.

When you want your children to do their homework, what is your approach? In all likelihood, you explain how important a good education is in today's world.

Are we all salespeople?

You bet we are!

Define Your Idea

An elderly lady, famous for her charitable work, inherited $1,000. She immediately sent $300 to the Red Cross, $300 to the Heart Fund, and $300 to the March of Dimes. Wondering how best to dispose of the final $100, she met a shabbily dressed man on the street and pressed the $100 into his trembling hand. With a warm smile, she whispered, "Good luck," and hurried on.

Two days later there was a knock on the lady's door. It was the same man.

"Do you want to see me?" she asked, touched by his display of gratitude.

"Yeah, lady," he said. "I had a heck of a time running you down, but here's your two grand. Good Luck came in and paid nineteen to one."

Whether or not the story is true, it points up what can happen when you don't define your ideas!

Another story that *is* true shows how the misinterpretation of one word changed the course of history.

In July 1945 the Emperor of Japan was ready to surrender to the Allies. So was his cabinet, but it wanted some time to discuss the terms of the Potsdam ultimatum. A press release was prepared announcing a policy of *mokusatsu*. Now *mokusatsu* has two meanings: to ignore and to refrain from comment. When the press release got on the foreign wires, it reached the Allies as, "The cabinet *ignores* the demand to surrender." What the Japanese really meant was: "The cabinet *has no comment at this time* on the demand to surrender."

Had the intended meaning been clear, the cabinet might have endorsed the emperor's decision to surrender. The unthinkable loss of face associated with issuing a correction forced Japan to abide by an erroneous translation.

One word, misinterpreted.

Although the misunderstanding in this case centered about the translation of a word from one language into another, the same kind of misunderstanding can occur between two people using the identical language. For example, a man was asked to give a recommendation for one of his former employees. He wrote, "I've known Ms. Davis for six years and I cannot recommend her too highly."

Was he recommending Ms. Davis?

Are you sure?

The crucial first point in selling an idea is to know what you want to say.

Basic stuff? Maybe. But you would be amazed how many people start talking before their idea has crystallized in their own mind. They confuse the blurred shadow of a thought for an idea, and their confusion becomes evident as soon as they open their mouth.

On the other hand, once you *understand* what you want to say, in nine cases out of ten you have little difficulty finding the appropriate words with which to express it. There is a good reason for that. Words are merely symbols for things. Most of us know the right words for the many things in our lives (this is a *book,* that is a *lamp,* the feeling I have is called *curiosity,* and so on). The trouble starts when we haven't completely visualized the things we want to put into words.

If you have ever said, "I *know* what I mean, but I just can't seem to find the words," then you are familiar with this frustrating experience. But the truth is, if you cannot find the words, you really don't *know* what you mean. Few of us lack the actual vocabulary with which to express our thoughts. Our real problem is to pull the things in our minds into focus and see them sharply so that we may choose the proper word-symbols for them.

So before you try to sell your idea, make very sure that you know precisely, concretely, and beyond doubt what it is.

Selling Your "Product"

Ask anyone in sales. He'll confirm it: you can have the finest product in the world and know your prospect's psyche as well as you know the geography of your living room, but if you fail to persuade him that it is somehow to his advantage to own what you are selling, the result is a foregone conclusion: no sale.

Question: How, precisely, do you convince him?

Simple. Just answer the crucial question in your prospect's mind.

The first lesson every salesperson learns is that people don't buy *things;* they buy what things will *do* for them. They buy enjoyment, fulfillment, satisfaction, solutions to problems, performance, advantages—in short, benefits.

A prospect for a furnace doesn't give a hoot about the thermodynamics of a heating plant. What he really wants to know is "Will it heat my home economically?"

He won't dream of reaching for his wallet, no matter how enthusiastically a salesperson informs him, "We add aluminum glycinate and magnesium carbonate to our acetylsalicylic acid!" He will only consider spending his money when he is told, "This headache tablet won't upset your stomach because these compounds combat certain side effects of aspirin."

For whether a prospect articulates it or not, the one crucial question always on his mind. is, "What's in it for *me*?" Until he receives a convincing answer, he will not buy.

So don't ask your boss to accept your idea for what it is; ask him to accept it for what it will *do* for him: Cut his costs; make him, his department, or his company more productive; reduce errors; build sales; boost profits; improve safety; whatever.

Want your boss to retool part of the production line? Don't describe how a new piece of machinery works and stop there. Go on to explain how it will slash waste, speed up production time, add to profitability.

No matter what kind of ideas you deal in, translate their features into benefits for your prospects—and watch your "sales" zoom.

Demonstrate Your Belief in the Idea

From your own experience with salespeople, you know it isn't difficult to spot the person who believes in his or her product and the one who doesn't. The true believer speaks with conviction. His eyes mirror his sincerity. His enthusiasm is infectious. And because these things are so, you are tempted to buy, and often do. The other person, by comparison, is dull and unconvincing.

During World War II, social psychologist R. K. Merton studied the techniques of mass persuasion. In the course of his investigations, he questioned people to get their reactions to Kate Smith's highly successful war-bond-selling campaign, during which she broadcast continuously for eighteen hours.

The characteristic cited most often, and approved most highly, by Miss Smith's audience was her sincerity. A typical comment was, "She *really means* what she says." Even though she frequently appeared on commercially sponsored programs and engaged in many of the same promotional activities as other radio stars, the public felt that in carrying out the bond drive, Kate Smith was interested only in the national welfare and did not care about any personal publicity that might accrue to her in the process. The marathon effort itself, suggests Dr. Merton, undoubtedly contributed to her reputation as a sincere, unselfish person.

The moral for anyone interested in the psychology of persuasion is clear: If you can convince your audience that *you* believe in what you are about to say, they are more likely to stay tuned in to your message and be persuaded by it.

How can you achieve this "belief in your belief"? In two important ways.

First, think it through. Unless you yourself believe in the value of your message, you cannot expect others to. A vague hope that what you have to say isn't worth listening to, a suspicion that it isn't practical, a half-admitted shortcoming—reservations like these in your own mind are reflected in your voice and demeanor.

Solution: Know beforehand that your idea is good.

How? Sell yourself on its benefits. Ask yourself if it will produce the results you promise. Step into your prospect's shoes. If someone else explained it to you, would you be convinced? Why? Are you sure?

Okay. Once you believe in it, nature will take care of the rest. Your belief will be written on your face, your voice, your posture. As a result, you will, almost automatically, be confident. People generally take you at your own value. Let them know you don't think much of your proposal and they'll agree. Let them know you are convinced that your idea has merit—and they'll agree with that too . . . until you prove otherwise.

Unless you keep people interested in what you want to tell them, you won't "sell" them a thing. For that reason, it's vital that you arrest their attention with the hope of hearing something of importance or help to them.

There is a world of difference between prefacing an idea with "Here, for what it's worth . . . " and "I've examined the situation from every possible angle, and this is what I feel we should do . . ."

One caution, however: Never try to bluff people into believing something that isn't true. You may fool them once, even twice, but they won't be victimized a third time. If you can't truthfully show confidence in your idea, it probably isn't worth selling.

Prove Your Case

When you come right down to it, salespeople deal in promises. They claim that their products will do a better job than other brands, deliver more value for the money, save time, make daily living more pleasurable. Implicit in each presentation is the statement, "What I am telling you is true."

But the public has grown skeptical of such claims. Consequently, the salesperson must be prepared to back up his promises with evidence that his prospect can believe. Through trial and error, men and women in sales have discovered that certain kinds of proof are most effective. While you may not be able to adapt all their techniques to your needs, here are several that you can use.

Visual Evidence.   After talking about the benefits of carrying a policy with his firm, the insurance agent whips out a photostat of a check made out for $750 to Mr. Charles Carter and says, "Mr. Carter collects this every month of his life because he had the foresight to prepare for his retirement twenty years ago. Wouldn't you like to have the same dependable protection?" It's a potent sales clincher.

As an idea person, you can use the same technique. Should you want to emphasize the importance of using a certain piece of safety equipment, for example, you might show your employees some photographs of workers who scoffed at the idea and sustained injuries. A picture of a person with an arm in a sling is worth ten thousand words of warning.

If you want to convince your boss that your assembly line has grown obsolete, you might show him a chart that dramatizes its low output as opposed to that of a newly revamped line in anther plant.

Photographs, slides, sketches, and diagrams can also back up the point you want to make. Keep them uncomplicated and easy to grasp, never more than one point to an exhibit. If you have several points to make, give each one its own picture.

Demonstration.   The encyclopedia sales representative says that his are the most up-to-date reference books available. To prove it, he turns to the article "Outer Space." Sure enough, our latest space explorations are described. He invites you to look up any subject; when you do, you discover that he's right; it is current.

Few sales techniques are so effective as a good demonstration, a fact every seller of ideas should take to heart. Your prospect may not be convinced by anything you *say,* but he cannot deny the testimony of his own eyes, for "seeing is believing."

Suppose you want to "sell" your boss on the idea of using a new machine. It's easier to operate than the old one, you tell him, and will save valuable time to boot because it does several operations simultaneously. He is reluctant to "buy" what you claim, primarily because he is used to the traditional machine, so you invite him to witness a contest. Let an employee run the old machine for ten minutes while you run the new one. Then he can see whether what you claim is true. Your challenge is accepted. When you turn out six feet of tubing to your competitor's four feet, you rest your case.

The person who can *show* his boss that what he says is true has the most convincing evidence of all.

The Testimony of Experts. The metals sales rep shows the buyer for a welding firm a statement signed by the chief engineer of a large company. It says that the sales rep's new alloy easily meets the company's rigid specifications for toxic vapor. The buyer is sufficiently impressed to place a trial order.

Whether we admit it or not, we tend to respect the testimony of "experts," those people who—because of their knowledge, status, or experience—are accepted as authorities in their field. The testimony of such people is rightly taken as evidence.

Assume that your proposal is to reduce drastically the company's planned plant expansion program over the next ten years. The plan has been in place for some time and reflects a lot of high-level thinking. You argue that it was based on old input and obsolete assumptions; it did not take certain recent technological advances into account—component miniaturization, for example.

The person you are trying to convince is unswayed. After all, it's your idea, so naturally *you* think it's good. But why should *he?*

So you use another tack. You show him an article by a prominent consulting engineer that surveys the technology of your industry. It traces the evolution of component miniaturization and predicts vast changes in how your products will be fabricated in the 1990s. Among other things. it states that one plant in 1990 will be able to turn out the volume now produced by four plants. The consultant has no ax to grind; he is an outsider citing facts. Your boss wavers, convinced that your idea at least merits serious consideration.

Somebody once defined an expert as "just another guy from out of town." But his recommendations frequently carry a special impact. Don't overlook him and the help he can give you.

Statistics. The mutual-fund sales rep shows you the figures. Over the last ten years, her fund has appreciated 90 percent. For every $100 invested a decade ago, her clients now own shares worth $190. On the average, money put into her fund has grown at the rate of 9 percent a year—half again what it can earn in a bank! Of course, she can't guarantee this will continue, but past performance is a fair indicator of future prospects. It sounds very good indeed.

Some prospects, and virtually all technical people, are peculiarly susceptible to statistical proof. They like figures. They trust figures. They think in terms of figures. If you can quote chapter and verse on such facts as costs, requirements, and the ultimate payout of your idea, you have the most convincing evidence of all.

Establish a Deadline

The introduction of a time element can often help persuade a prospect to buy your idea. No one likes to miss an opportunity. If you can show a prospect that he must seize your proposition immediately in order to realize maximum benefits from it, he will tend to dismiss the minor reservations that are preventing him from accepting your idea.

Perhaps the timing of your idea is crucial to success. Possibly, in order to implement it, a number of suppliers must be lined up. Maybe the cost of certain equipment is due to rise soon. Whatever the "deadlines" inherent in your idea, take this opportunity to inventory them. Here is a checklist of possible reasons why your prospect should decide in your favor *now:*

Impending shortages of certain materials
Imminent price rise

Seasonal considerations
Length of lead time required
Immediate tax advantages
Loss of savings (or profits) through procrastination
Availability of manpower
Especially favorable delivery schedules
Strong market demand
Competitive considerations

Don't Forget to "Ask for the Order"

Leaving a courthouse where he had listened to a colleague in action one day, famed attorney Clarence Darrow was heard muttering to himself, "The fool! The fool!" Asked why he was so upset, Darrow explained. The lawyer had done everything perfectly. He came to court prepared. He pointed out blatant contradictions in the prosecution's case. He presented telling evidence on behalf of his client. "He did everything as I would have," Darrow said, "except for one thing. He didn't ask for the dismissal of charges against his client. The *fool!*"

Many people commit the same error. They take infinite pains in working out the details of their idea. They present it clearly. They even manage to excite their audience. Then they stop short of the realization of their goal. *They don't ask for what they want.*

Your listener may be genuinely excited about your idea yet may do nothing about it simply because you neglect to explain where he fits in. What do you want him to do? Give his approval? Sign a paper? Arrange an appointment for you? Make a telephone call? Introduce you to someone? Strike a gong? What?

Tell him.

Be Prepared to Fight Inertia

One of the most exasperating objections in the prospect's all-too-full arsenal is, "We're satisfied with our present method [product, process, strategy, etc.]. Why should we change?" Backed by arguments on behalf of current benefits enjoyed and the inconveniences of disrupting routine, these words are too often accepted as final by proponents of a new idea.

How do you, the advocate of a new idea, overcome prospect inertia?

There are valid, tested, and convincing ways. Approaches vary, but the essential strategy remains the same: When your prospect pleads satisfaction, you must sell him constructive dissatisfaction.

Create a New Standard. Frequently, the "satisfied" person is simply unaware that a better method or product is available. So look for the "hidden benefits" in your idea. Will it simplify procedures? Result in a safer work environment? Reduce errors? Explain why.

Change the Frame of Reference. People tend to grow rigid in their thinking, to see things in very limited terms: price, safety, convenience, and so on. Introduce *another* factor for consideration, thereby altering the frame of reference, and you may break through your prospect's resistance. For example: "True, this machine turns out our widgits at a profit today. But will it continue to do so in 1990, when our volume requirements will be 80 percent higher?" "The old product is sturdy enough, but this new lightweight alloy will slash shipping costs in half without sacrificing quality."

Introduce the Ultimate Factor: Cost. Prove that your idea will cost less in the long run, and you have a powerful argument on its behalf. Often, you can do this by citing the hidden savings implicit in your idea. For instance, will your idea reduce warehousing requirements, idle inventory, worker inefficiency and error, customer dissatisfaction? Develop the knack of tracing the cost ramifications of the way things are now done, then examine your idea with a view toward pinpointing the costs it can eliminate or reduce.

From the Laboratory. As much as you can learn about selling from salespeople, they are not the only source of information available. A lot of facinating selling know-how has emerged from the laboratory too.

For example, in presenting your case, should you offer your strongest argument first or last? When, if ever, should your listener's fears be built into reasons for accepting your viewpoint? Should you ever admit a negative fact about your idea or proposition?

Some startling answers to these and other questions about persuasion emerged when a group of social scientists, working under a grant from the Rockefeller Foundation, examined the effects of different tactics on human psychology. For anyone who deals with others, the results of the experiments offer a gold mine of down-to-earth, psychological know-how. Reached under laboratory conditions, they are neither colored by personal bias not slanted by a single individual experience. They are tested, measured, proven.

Climax Versus Anticlimax

Question: Is it better to open your case with your strongest argument or to save it for the close?

Answer: Tests showed that the presentation of your major argument at the outset (anticlimax order) will be most effective where the listener is initially little interested in the message. The reason: It arouses his interest and motivates him to "learn" what is being said.

Where the listener is particularly interested in your message in the first place (for example, if he has asked you for information), you are better off saving your major argument for the close (climax order). The reason: The listener's initial curiosity is sufficient to carry him through the opening portions of your remarks. After several minutes, should interest and attention begin to wane, you can renew them with your most impressive reason for adopting the course of action you are advocating.

Can You Afford to Give Both Sides of Your Story?

Many people, committed to the power-of-positive-thinking approach, argue that bringing up negative points about an idea is certain death. "Talk yes, get yes." they contend.

Here's news from the researchers: Experiments prove that with at least three types of people, you will stand a better chance of winning approval of your proposition by deliberately bringing up the *negative* points about it, as well as the positive. Which types of people? *(a)* the educated one; *(b)* the person who disagrees with you at the very outset; and *(c)* the person who is exposed to subsequent arguments against your idea from others.

On the other hand, exactly the opposite strategy is recommended when *(a)* the person is uneducated; *(b)* the person agrees right off with your viewpoint; or *(c)* the person is not likely to be exposed to counterarguments. In their cases, the studies show, it's best to stay strictly positive.

In a nutshell: If you are trying to convince someone who is likely to be approached by others competing for his approval, you can largely neutralize their arguments by anticipating—and answering—them in advance. In effect, you arm your listener with reasons for ignoring or discounting the arguments he will hear against your idea. Thus "inoculated," he will tend to retain the positive conclusions you have planted in his mind; in fact, he is likely to take pleasure in resisting others with reasons he has already accepted as convincing.

When to Admit Limitations

Two groups of people were exposed to identical presentations on the benefits and drawbacks of a common household product—with one small difference. Group A was *first* informed of the advantages of owning the product, *then* told of the drawbacks. This order was reversed with group B. Several weeks later, both groups of individuals were questioned. Group A had bought almost twice as much of the product as group B.

Psychologists call this the primacy effect. That is, what a person hears first lingers with him longest. If you list the benefits of an idea before the drawbacks, you create a positive "that's for me" state of mind. Start with the drawbacks and create an attitude of resistance.

For example, if your plan to streamline office procedure is expensive, you might admit the drawback to your boss in this way: "My plan will free one secretary and two clerk-typists for more important work and save us over $3,000 a year by eliminating many duplicate records, even though it's a little expensive to set into action." The benefits "smother" the drawback.

Is It Safe to Let Your Listener Draw His Own Conclusions?

The researchers discovered that the answer to this question depends on two factors:

1. Does your proposition involve the listener personally? Or impersonally?
2. Is your proposition a simple one? Or is it complicated?

Thus, when the listener is highly educated or intimately familiar with the subject, it is unnecessary to spell out the conclusion for him. In fact, he is likely to be insulted by your presumption in drawing diagrams. An engineer, for instance, needn't spell things out for the boss with a strong technical training, though she may have to be quite detailed for the one without such a background. An insurance sales rep need not map for a banker the major advantages of creating an immediate estate, but he may very well have to itimize them for an architect.

When the idea or proposition is an ego-involving one (dealing with the listener's opinion of himself), the listener is strongly motivated to make up his own mind. When the idea is an impersonal one, however, the listener tends to welcome conclusion drawing by the speaker.

Complexity is another factor. If the benefits of an idea are obvious, emphasis on them by the speaker makes little difference. On the other hand, if they are involved (hidden tax benefits, for example) and the steps leading from the premises to the desired conclusion are not immediately obvious, the speaker should spell out in detail the benefits he is offering.

Fear: Your Friend or Foe?

"Suppose our competitors maintain their current prices?"

"Unless you order now, I can't guarantee delivery by the twenty-fifth."

"You wouldn't want to risk personal injury, would you?"

Much effective persuasion is based on a threat, hidden or obvious. But just how powerful a convincer *is* the old-fashioned scare? What are its limitations?

While much remains to be learned in this area, a good deal is already known about the efficacy of threat appeals in persuasion. The research group found, for example, that three things occur when a person is exposed to a threat appeal. He wonders if it will happen to him. He grows tense. And his tension is reduced as he listens to the speaker explain how to avert the threat. Most important, this reduction of tension operates as a *reinforcement* of the speaker's recommendations.

However, there are three built-in pitfalls in the threat approach.

Each of us is equipped with a kind of unconscious blackout system. When we experience something too oppressive for comfort, we drop a curtain over it. Therefore, if you create *too* much anxiety, your listener will simply tune you out; he'll stop taking seriously what he hears because it is too painful. (Case in point: confirmed cigarette smokers.)

Another danger of this approach is that sometimes, when the threat creates more anxiety than we can tolerate, we react with aggression toward the source of the threat. For example, we reject or refuse to believe the speaker's statements. We may even form a deep personal dislike for him (and, if he is a sales representative, for his company).

In short, the threat is a powerful tool of persuasion—up to a point. Past that point, it ceases to persuade at all; it simply paralyzes. The word: moderation.

Should Your Listener Get into the Act?

The psychologists' answer: an unqualified yes!

But what if you are selling an intangible—or an idea with long-range benefits? It's obviously one thing to get a person to test-drive a car or hammer a piece of unbreakable glass or use a tool. But how can you get a potential user of a new production idea into the act?

There *is* a way; it is powerful, convincing, and practically surefire.

It's called verbal conformity. Put simply, the psychologists discovered that saying is believing. If you can get a person to repeat all, or a part, of your argument in his own words, the simple act of saying will influence his private convictions. Several methods for achieving this verbal conformity suggest themselves. A salesperson might ask his prospect to explain the proposition to his wife, partner, or colleague. An employee might suggest that her boss dictate a memo on the subject. A shrewd manager might even purposely grope for words, allowing a subordinate to fill them in. The point is to get your listener talking.

There are three vital advantages to this technique: The listener invariably puts the message into his own words, thus picturing more clearly in his own mind the benefit images you are trying to create. The words he chooses are those that have the most emotionally loaded meanings for him. And by encouraging him to put them in his own terms, the persuader boosts the odds that at a later date some reinforcing situation will occur to remind the listener of the presentation.

For instance, suppose insurance agent Smith doesn't know that prospect Jones would like to assure a substantial donation to his alma mater. By permitting Jones to put the benefits of increased insurance into his own words, Smith may get Jones to say to Mrs. Jones, "This extra insurance would be a wonderful way to do something for the university." Having said that, days after Smith has departed, Jones will think of the increased insurance whenever he receives literature from his school, drops in at his university club, or discusses college life with friends. They represent "reinforcing" situations.

A word of caution: Make very sure that your listener understands your message clearly before he puts it into his own words, for experiments indicate that if he bungles his "performance," he grows dissatisfied with himself and transfers to the message his inadequacy in explaining it. If his performance satisfies him, the message tends to satisfy—and to persuade.

Does Repetition Pay Off?

Only up to a certain point. A message—any message—is remembered better if it's heard twice instead of once, three times instead of twice, four times instead of three times. But according to the results of intensive experiments, there is little improvement in the listener's retention of your story after the fourth repetition.

So if you haven't convinced after the fourth approach, lay off for a while, then go back and start over.

Different People, Different Tactics

Persons low in self-esteem and self-confidence tend to be the most easily persuaded. They unconsciously seek the approval of others, whom they automatically accept as superior to themselves.

And who is the individual with the greatest sales resistance? The nervous, neurotic, habitually suspicious person.

Further, say the researchers, persons of high intelligence or good education tend to be swayed less easily by emotional appeals than by impressive logic supported by acceptable proofs.

People of low intelligence respond more readily to emotional appeals, are less critical, less easily moved by logical arguments.

Whether the product is a diesel-powered locomotive or a new idea, there is nothing very mysterious about the process involved in selling it: A has a need; B has the means to fulfill that need; A buys from B. Result: a mutually profitable transaction.

But A doesn't always *know* that he has a need, and that's where salesmanship and the psychology of persuasion come into play. It is up to you, the salesperson, to demonstrate to your prospect that *(a)* the need exists; *(b)* your idea will answer the need; and *(c)* applying your idea to his need will result in some worthwhile benefit to him.

That, in a nutshell, is what the ability to persuade others is all about. And it is one of the indisputable hallmarks of those who move up in the world.

11

Managing Creativity

People are 95 percent alike. They share the same basic wants, needs, and yearnings: food, shelter, clothing, safety. They raise families, enjoy the company of others, seek a little pleasure, try to find a place in the world.

It is the unique 5 percent of their makeup that differentiates one person from another, the saint from the sinner, the towering intellectual from the dullard, the leader from the led.

Since we are basically the same physically, what gives us individuality must be found elsewhere. Call it what you will—mind, spirit, personality —there is something intangible but nevertheless real that makes Bob Smith different from Joe Jones and Mary Brown different from Susan Green. And it is these differences—in talent, temperament, interests, attitudes, ambitions, and values—among employees that make the manager's job so challenging.

Nowhere, perhaps, are these differences so evident as in the area of creativity.

What Is Creativity?

There is no completely satisfactory definition of creativity. What, after all, do Michaelangelo, Henry Ford, Laurence Olivier, and the man who solves a tricky manufacturing problem have in common? A high IQ? Vaulting imagination? Curiosity? Inordinate patience? Stubbornness? A little, or a lot, of each of these things? No one really knows, although many have tried to isolate the individual components of original thought. The problem is that no matter what sort of list is drawn up, exceptions to the rules immediately come to mind.

Nevertheless, creative people do tend to have certain things in common, and the manager who wishes to get the best out of such employees would be well advised to understand what makes them tick, the kind of environment they thrive in, how to adjust your needs to theirs. A sub-

139

sidiary benefit is the strong likelihood that, in the course of providing the kind of management atmosphere in which originality can flourish, you increase your chances of encouraging more creativity not only from the relatively few with a strong predisposition for originality but from *all* your people.

The first question that suggests itself is, Is that desirable? After all, many jobs seem to require precious little creative thought. Why rock the boat?

There are three answers. First, there isn't a job you can name that cannot be done better in some way, whether it's more quickly, more accurately, or less wastefully. Employees who understand that you welcome fresh ideas will seek them out. Second, even if an employee whose creativity is encouraged cannot find ways to do his own job more effectively, he may identify some altogether unrelated area where improvements can be made. Creativity is not easily confined or compartmentalized; it tends to spill over and surprise. Third—and this may be the most overlooked factor of all—approaching work with a creative attitude makes that work interesting and enjoyable. On the surface many jobs appear cut and dried. Viewed creatively, they can be transformed into tantalizing challenges. And what challenges and teases us is almost always more interesting than what does not.

If we agree, then, that creativity in employees is desirable and ought to be fostered, how do we recognize it?

Creative talent manifests itself in many ways. One person may possess an uncanny ability for solving mechanical problems. Another may be able to identify weaknesses in someone else's ideas. A third may have a genius for managing resources. Who can say which one is most creative?

As a rule of thumb, creativity may be defined as any activity that results in something new or different that is ultimately beneficial to someone. It may be a theory, artistic creation, invention, process, solution to a problem, or any of a thousand things. It may range from applying an old idea to a new situation, to the promulgation of a totally unprecedented view of the universe. But in one way or another, its product is something that did not exist before.

How Creative People Tick

The very word *creativity* conjurs up images of the handful of giants who have shaped our world—Plato, Aristotle, Descartes, Jefferson,

Shakespeare, Curie, Einstein, Freud, and so on. Certainly, those names suggest lives devoted to high intellectual pursuits, and there is no comparison between founding a school of philosophy and contriving a new way to manufacture widgits. But in both instances virtually the same creative process is at work. There is, first of all, dissatisfaction with the status quo. A problem or need is identified. There is a search for possible answers; a great deal of random thinking, both conscious and unconscious; a gradual narrowing of focus on essentials; experimentation with possible solutions; and, finally, the pinpointing of the best possible answer.

Almost by definition, creative people are unique, for they ask questions no one has asked before. Nevertheless, they do share a number of common characteristics. Not *all* creative people, to be sure, share *all* these traits, but they tend to have most of the following in common.

Drive. Creative people are highly self-motivated. Nothing galvanizes them so much as a challenge. Once intrigued by a problem, they can summon enormous bursts of energy and concentration for long periods of time in their pursuit of answers. They will eat, drink, and breathe the problem at hand, talking and thinking of nothing else. A kind of monomania sets in, and any demands on their time that drag them away from the problem or project are viewed with loathing. They want to be left alone to wrestle with the challenge.

Perseverance. The more creative a person, the higher his or her frustration tolerance. Thomas Edison's patience was legendary. He never viewed an experiment that failed as a waste of time. Rather, his attitude was, "Well, that's one approach I needn't try again." Once convinced that finding the answer is worthwhile, a creator will take infinite pains and whatever time is necessary to conclude his work successfully.

Curiosity. Creative people like to know the whys, whats, and wherefores of things. They are nosy, inquisitive, eclectic. Brief answers seldom satisfy them, and the more complete the answers they get, the more questions they come up with.

Wide Interests. Because they are curious, creative people are interested in many things aside from their specialties and read widely outside their fields. The truly inventive engineer, for instance, may also study judo, marine biology, music, gourmet cooking, and ways to beat the blackjack dealer in gambling casinos. At social gatherings, creative people will frequently buttonhole those in different lines of work and assault them with questions about their jobs. They are receptive to new information, fresh ideas, outlandish theories, novel ways of looking at things, for they never know when something they see or hear may trigger an idea that they can use.

Self-confidence. Creative people have great belief in themselves and their ability to overcome obstacles. They also have a high sense of their own worth. Indeed, they may appear to possess towering egos and, to be sure, some do. But it is often less a case of egotism than belief in the power of approaching problems positively, as if failure were out of the question. Charles Kettering, for example, wanted to make an electric starter for automobiles, but every engineer showed him why he couldn't possibly do it. A motor powerful enough to turn a gasoline engine would be as big as the engine and need a battery as big as the car. He tried many approaches before it occured to him that maybe that answer was false. He didn't want to turn the engine by the motor very long—just for a few seconds, to start it. Every engineer assumed the need for a motor and battery big enough for continuous load. Kettering saw that the load would be only momentary; so he designed a small motor and battery that would turn the engine for only a second or two, just long enough to start it.

Observation. Generally, creative people see things that others do not—similarities, analogies, parallels. When working on an idea, they have a knack for considering everything they see, read, and experience in terms of, "How can I use that? Can it be adapted, modified, or combined with something else to solve my problem?" There is a ceaseless search for new applications of old principles.

Imagination. Most creative men and women live in a world of "Suppose I did this? Why not do it this way?" They continually play with ideas and notions, dismissing nothing until they're convinced it is of no value.

Intuition. Creative people are often impelled to act on a hunch. True, their hunches are almost always based on an amalgam of forgotten experience and unfettered imagination, but they get feelings that cannot be explained away intellectually. Many highly creative people have referred to this phenomenon. Albert Einstein: "At times I feel certain I am right while not knowing the reason." Irving Langmuir, Nobel laureate in chemistry: "It is absurd to think that reason should be our guide in all cases. Reason is too slow and too difficult . . . . We underrate the importance of intuition." Thomas Edison: "The key to successful methods comes right out of the air. A real, new thing like an idea, a beautiful melody, is pulled out of space."

Sense of Humor. As you might suspect, people who are adept at seeing similarities between dissimilar things and extracting general principles from concrete instances also enjoy the surprise in a funny story, the unexpected twist in a clever pun, the irreverence that is part of humor. Wit, which largely depends on the startling juxtaposition of dissimilar ideas, appeals to them. And, of course, humor helps them deal with the failures that are necessary preludes to success in the creative process.

Idiosyncrasy. Not surprisingly, people who are unconventional in their thinking are frequently also unconventional in their behavior. They may dress differently from their peers, be chronically late for appointments, ignore standard operating procedures. True, some very pedestrian people affect these external signs of being different, and not every eccentric is creative, but more often than not, creative people *do* march to a different drummer, and it shows in their behavior.

Lest these characteristics give the impression that creative people are a breed apart, not subject to the same motivations and laws as lesser mortals, let's recognize that in addition to the above, they can also be lazy, uncooperative, sullen, jealous, unproductive, petty, ornery, and frustrating to work with. What chiefly differentiates them from others are a few extra wrinkles in their brains. Those wrinkles make a big difference, but they do not represent grounds for amnesty in advance for boorish, uncooperative, or prima-donna-like behavior. Something to bear in mind.

The Creative Climate

Given such people, in what kind of environment might they be expected to thrive? What do they require in order to mine their own creativity most effectively?

The first need is to be alone, at least part of the time, in order to think. A man or woman in the grip of a perplexing problem needs solitude to summon whatever inner resources may be necessary to solve the problem. Almost universally, idea people report getting their best ideas in solitude—while driving, raking leaves, baking bread, and the like. There appears to be a very real need to be removed from distractions, particularly noise and movement. This is not to say that a creator must work in a vacuum, but he should have several quiet hours daily at his disposal. No truly great idea ever emerged from a committee.

A second need is for unstructured time. Although it is close to blasphemy in the Western ethic to do nothing, inactivity appears to be a prerequisite for creativity. Brain activity is invisible to the naked eye, and the person who to all outward appearances is daydreaming may be in the throes of working out a complex problem. Most good ideas are the result of slow simmering, a period of gestation during which memory, experience, imagination, and fantasy are allowed to work their magic.

A third need is naïveté, a kind of pristine gullibility that suspends judgment and rules out criticism. The ideal creative environment is free of rejection. For a period of time during the creative process, anything is considered within the realm of possibility—the suspension of the law of gravity, the transmutation of lead into gold, traveling faster than the speed of light, *anything*.

A fourth need is for a combination of alertness and discipline. These are necessary prerequisites for all productive work, of course, but they assume a particular importance in the creative act. They are often the conditions that enable the creator to recognize—after a period of prolonged gestation—the existence of a particular similarity between two or more phenomena that had previously escaped notice. Translated into environmental terms, they require free time and good physical working conditions: adequate lighting and ventilation, the absence of distractions.

Additional needs vary from individual to individual. Some people get their best ideas while soaking in a hot tub; others, while getting their hair cut. But the four conditions cited above appear to be the bedrock basics of the general climate most conducive to creativity.

Managing Creative People

If creative people are so special and require a hothouse environment worthy of an exotic orchid, how can a manager whose job is to get things done ever hope to manage them successfully? Must they continually be catered to, stroked, and treated differently from others? If the creators are given free rein to put their feet up on their desks, gaze dreamily into space, and simply think, what will happen to productivity, not to mention morale?

Clearly, needs differ from situation to situation. If you are managing an R and D installation where creativity is the mission and one good idea can ultimately be worth millions of dollars to your company, the answer is most definitely give your creative people everything they need. If you manage a department responsible for so much output per week, month, or quarter, obviously you must find a happy compromise between encouraging originality and getting the work done. You must decide the relative importance of creativity to your major responsibilities and how much time and effort can be prudently invested in promoting inventiveness. It's a quesiton of priorities.

Ideally, however, here are some guidelines for managing creative people. Bearing in mind the realities of your own situation—head count, resources, mission—use them as common sense dictates.

Establish a Colleague Relationship. Creative people are more achievement oriented than company oriented. Their loyalty is to their profession, not to the organization that pays their salary. They bridle at rules and regulations that they view as interfering with the pursuit of ideas. It is useless to tell them, "Do it this way because that's the way we do things here." The manager accustomed to having his way simply because he's the manager and because subordinates are supposed to obey their managers is due for a shock. The creator could not care less for titles, so don't hide behind yours and thunder *diktats* from Mount Olympus; rather, explain with facts and logic why he should do something, and he'll listen with respect. What he seeks and responds to is not the conventional boss-subordinate relationship but a colleague relationship, based on freewheeling discussion and constructive criticism. If you confront him with unilateral decisions requiring unquestioning obedience, he will either tune you out or else go his merry way to a company he finds more compatible.

Suspend Critical Judgment. A good idea is sometimes hampered in its early stages because the form in which it is initially expressed is weak and unconvincing. The originator may not be able to sell an idea or may not yet have worked out all the bugs. But don't confuse the presentation with the idea itself. A chemist with only a so-so ability to explain things may pop up with the ideal solution to a problem in distillation. The painfully shy accountant who stutters could produce a new way to finance your expansion program. Even really offbeat ideas may contain the germ of solid thinking—if you can separate the wheat from the chaff. That's why it is important that you view every idea as a potential winner. Granted, to turn an idea into usable shape, you may have to add, subtract, modify, or combine it with additional ideas. In such a case the original idea may, in retrospect, become merely a jumping-off point. But without it, you would get nowhere. Be slow, therefore, to condemn any idea to oblivion. If it is not feasible today, it may be eminently practicable tomorrow or next year. Even if it appears unusable, the "secret ingredient" needed to transform it into solid gold may pop up in the future. Help make his idea work and the creator will be in your debt.

Establish Mutually Acceptable Deadlines.   Most people work best against deadlines, and creative people are no exception. In fact, because they are apt to grow enamored of a particular problem to the exclusion of all other considerations, creators are prone to piddle away their time in endless elaborations and refinements of an idea. Deadlines establish a sense of urgency that compels them to keep on track. If a project is large or complicated, interim deadlines that require progress reports may also be necessary. But deadlines that are set arbitrarily—or appear to be— will probably be ignored. To assure cooperation, meet with the individual at the start of a job and reach agreement on goals, budget limitations, resources available, how long it should take, interim dates for progress reports, and a firm date for completion.

Maintain Contact.   Although a manager shouldn't breathe down a creative employee's neck during a project, good supervision is critical to any person's productivity. Use those interim dates and checkpoints on the work schedule to talk over unexpected problems that may be holding up progress.

Give Them a Chance to Fail.   Failure is a recognized stepping-stone toward ultimate success in the creative process, but it's anathema to the businessman, who necessarily bears a "bottom line" responsibility. The manager of creative people must go out of his way to be supportive during the trying period of failure and demonstrate that he doesn't consider it the end of the world. If he doesn't, fear of failure may prevent true initiative. A few words of encouragement, a suggestion as to how to proceed or whom to talk to, or just simply listening can pay big dividends in the long run.

Grant Them Some Time Off.   We have already seen that creative people need solitude. Some of the best ideas come during idle periods immediately following stretches of intense concentration. Sudden insights frequently emerge from a subconscious mind that, until recently, was totally occupied. Since ideas are often born in the least likely circumstances and places, it is less important for the creator to be in a certain place at a certain time than it is to work under optimum conditions. An occasional "Take the rest of the day off" or "Why not work on it at home on Monday?" can go a long way toward increasing the productivity of creative people.

Give Recognition.   You like to get credit for your ideas. So do your creative people. Be quick, therefore, to show appreciation for good work and see to it that individuals receive the proper acknowledgment for their ideas, whether it takes the form of a bonus, prize, raise—or the simple, public expression, "Well done!"

Such rewards are not only just and proper; they are extremely practical. Recognition tends to raise employee standards. Next time they will try to equal or surpass the good job they did this time. And those who witness the recognition will be spurred on to greater effort. A little friendly competition never hurt anyone.

Bend the Rules.   Every organization has its regulations, but it also accumulates a lot of red tape over the years. Creative people usually detest paper work, going through channels, and all the other paraphernalia of bureaucracy. They can drive managers up the wall with their erratic ways, but once you understand the iron grip that the pursuit of an idea can have on them, you may be a bit more sympathetic toward their sense of priorities. Bearing in mind the needs of your company, when possible smooth their way by not insisting that they go by the book in every instance.

Don't Let Your Personal Needs Stifle Creativity.   There is no way of estimating how many good ideas have been stillborn because of managerial timidity. It can take many forms: "forget it"; "too impractical"; "can't possibly work"; "we've never done that before." There are three needs that frequently underlie a manager's reluctance to encourage originality. If any of them strikes a chord, it may be time to review your own mental set.

The Need for the Familiar. All of us are habit prone. We become attached to certain time-tested methods of performing various tasks. When something new is called for, a conflict arises between the old, accepted methods and different or untried modes of operation. The noncreative manager will usually stick to the time-proven methods, while the creative manager will actively seek new avenues of approach.

The Need for Excessive Order. Closely associated with the need to adhere to the familiar is this creative barrier. Managers afflicted with "hardening of the categories" accept only that information that fits preexisting classifications. They tend to reject new ideas that do not have a ready-made slot. On the other hand, the creative manager makes a conscious effort to ignore time-proven slots and examines a new idea strictly on its own merit.

The Need to Conform. This need is characterized by such feelings as "Curiosity killed the cat," "Bet on a sure thing," and "Better safe than sorry." The manager who believes in these aphorisms is expressing the exact opposite of the freedom from conformity.

This doesn't imply that to be creative is to make a concerted effort to be different for its own sake. It simply implies a willingness to take calculated risks and accept the possibility of being wrong.

Don't Be a Creativity Killer. Unwittingly, a lot of managers are idea killers. Some are snobs who think, "If Jones could dream up good ideas, she wouldn't be working for me in the first place." But everybody has to start someplace. Jones just might have the answer to a nagging problem. She deserves a hearing.

Others are so mundane in their own thinking that they are jealous of anyone who shows a spark of creativity.

Still others don't want to rock the boat. They view every idea as a threat to their own position and honestly, but erroneously, believe that theirs is the best of all possible worlds.

The solution? Take stock of yourself as a judge of ideas. If, upon analysis, you discover that you tend to quash ideas for any reason besides their lack of intrinsic merit, consciously try to suppress the personal prejudices that are costing you good ideas.

Creative people are a lot like everybody else, only more so. They tend to be more individualistic, more stubborn, more curious, more impatient with others, more enthusiastic, more demanding of themselves and the people with whom they come into contact. On the face of it, therefore, they are totally and irrevocably unmanageable.

Yet, treated with an understanding of what motivates them, how they tick, and what they require by way of a good working environment, they almost always emerge as a company's most valuable employees. They contribute more because they have more to contribute. The manager fortunate enough to have creative people reporting to him will find them among his greatest challenges; but at the same time he will discover that in the process of supervising them his own skills are constantly being tested, sharpened, and improved, for the real secret of managing creative people is creative management.

12

Dealing with People — Creatively

When you come right down to it, *all* good management is creative, for in order to deal successfully with his people, a manager must be a rare amalgam of sensitivity, empathy, humaneness, and good judgment. A fortunate few are born with these desirable qualities. But the majority must consciously acquire and cultivate them because employees differ widely in their specific ambitions, hopes, fears, dreams, and psychological needs. In order to communicate with them effectively, therefore, the manager needs to know how each individual ticks and what considerations motivate him.

What Makes People Act as They Do?

Before we consider your subordinates as employees, let's explore them as people subject to a certain hierarchy of needs and desires. Aside from the biological urges by which we are all driven—hunger, thirst, sex, the avoidance of pain—there are several common psychological denominators.

Nobody likes to think of himself as a faceless member of a group. We all crave recognition of our individuality by those whose esteem we value —our parents, children, friends, fellow workers, superiors. We enjoy thinking of ourselves as unique, unlike anyone who has ever existed in the past or will ever exist in the future—as indeed we are. The general civilian distaste for the military life is a familiar example of this aversion to dehumanization.

Another motivational factor is the desire to excel. Whether it goes back to our cave-dwelling ancestors, who had to beat the other fellow in order to survive, or some perverse urge in human nature to outperform others in order to prove our own worth to ourselves, the wish to do at least one thing better than most other people is a strong human trait.

Closely allied to the other desires, but somewhat different, is the desire for status—a need for external or symbolic proof of individual worth. It may take any of a hundred forms: a big house, a flashy car, an important-sounding title, a certificate or diploma, membership in an exclusive club. Admit it or not, almost all of us are victims of this passion for grown-up toys. We seem to need tangible proof of our achievements and station in life, whatever they may be.

Of course, these basic desires are not equally strong in all people. Some have a specially pronounced desire to excel and less need for status. Others have a less developed urge to excel but a strong need for recognition. But by and large you will not go far wrong if you assume that all people are, to some degree, driven by these desires.

What Employees Want Most

The manager who believes that he intuitively grasps the needs of his people may be in for a rude awakening. A pertinent study was conducted by a group of psychologists some years ago. They visited twenty-four industrial plants across the nation in order to measure employee attitudes toward various on-the-job morale items. Each worker interviewed was handed a list of ten items and asked to arrange them in what he or she considered their proper order of importance. Their supervisors were given the same list and asked to predict how their subordinates would answer.

Here is a chance to take the same test yourself. When you finish, match your answers with those given by the employees and the supervisors. While there are no correct answers, *how* you reply will tell you a lot about yourself: how much sympathy you have for the aspirations of others, your understanding of what motivates workers, your opinion of others—in short, your Management IQ.

In the spaces provided, enter the items by letter code in what you consider to be the descending order of importance to employees (most important consideration first, second most important consideration second, etc.).

A. Feeling "in on things"   1)____
B. Full appreciation of work done   2)____
C. Good wages   3)____
D. Good working conditions   4)____
E. Interesting work   5)____
F. Job security   6)____

G. Personal loyalty to workers   7)___
H. Promotion and growth in company   8)___
I. Sympathetic help with personal problems   9)___
J. Tactful disciplining   10)___

Now compare your list with these two:

How the Supervisors Assumed the Employees Would Answer	How the Employees Actually answered
1) **C**—Good wages	1) **B**—Full appreciation of work done
2) **F**—Job security	2) **A**—Feeling "in on things"
3) **H**—Promotion and growth in company	3) **I**—Sympathetic help with personal problems
4) **D**—Good working conditions	4) **F**—Job security
5) **E**—Interesting work	5) **C**—Good wages
6) **G**—Personal loyalty to workers	6) **E**—Interesting work
7) **J**—Tactful disciplining	7) **H**—Promotion and growth in company
8) **B**—Full appreciation of work done	8) **G**—Personal loyalty to workers
9) **I**—Sympathetic help with personal problems	9) **D**—Good working conditions
10) **A**—Feeling "in on things"	10) **J**—Tactful disciplining

Surprised?

The supervisors were dumbfounded!

Yet, they had worked with the people under them for anywhere from a few months to thirty-five years. They had talked with them, joked with them, even counted some of them among their close personal friends. Presumably, they knew what those people wanted.

Compare those lists again. It's difficult to see how the supervisors could have been more mistaken, isn't it?

How did you do? Does your list approximate the one drawn up by the workers or that of the supervisors? Did you list good wages either first or second, or did you realize intuitively that to a worker money is not the primary concern, important though it may be? Did you fall into the trap of assuming that employees respond most favorably to material rewards, or did you correctly predict their distinct preference for intangibles?

If you called all—or most—of your shots wrong, you can see how easy it is to think you know your people when, in reality, you do not.

The Self-Image

It is important to bear in mind that the results of the foregoing employee poll reflect the *average* of all the answers given, not any of the individual responses. Obviously, every single worker did not list the various items precisely in the order given. There were variations in each reply.

And that is understandable. Every person, including those who work under you, is an individual, with unique values, ambitions, and goals. The sum total of those values, ambitions, and goals (along with many other things, such as inherited characteristics and environmental influences) is reflected in the picture of himself that every person carries in his own mind. This picture, frequently referred to as his self-image, is a major clue to that person's psychological makeup.

One man, for example, may picture himself as the epitome of all the major virtues, a born leader, better than most people. Another person may view himself as possessed of a keen analytical mind, unswayed by emotional considerations. A third may entertain an image of himself as a great innovator and idea person.

As a general rule, people tend to respond positively to those external forces that corroborate their own opinions of themselves and negatively to those external forces that do not. So if you wanted three such people to wear their hard hats on the job, for example, you would be wise to approach them in terms of their individual self-image.

To the first, your most effective appeal might be, "Everybody looks up to you, Bill. If you made a point of wearing the hat, the others would follow your lead."

To the second, the best approach could be, "These hats have reduced head injuries more than 96 percent wherever they've been used in our industry, George. Don't you agree that they're worth using?"

The third person would be most apt to respond to this: "You're a bright guy, Jim. I don't have to draw pictures for you on the subject of safety. These hats have tested out, and we want all of you to take advantage of the latest safety equipment."

What have you really done in each case? You've put what you want done in terms of each person's self-image.

A bit childish? Perhaps. But it works.

Winning Cooperation

Despite your best intentions and efforts, however, sometimes your people will withhold their cooperation. There is seldom any single reason for their recalcitrance. One person will be uncooperative out of ignorance, another out of spite, a third to vent his own frustrations, a fourth because his teen-age daughter dented the car last night.

Nevertheless, there are certain recurring causes of employee uncooperativeness that every manager should be aware of and, ideally, eliminate by not allowing them to build up in the first place. If you took the trouble to analyze the reasons why your people don't always go along with your desires, you would probably find the culprit to be one of the following:

They Don't Understand What You Want. You cannot expect a subordinate to perform optimally if he is unsure what you expect of him. Garbled instructions, contradictory orders, uncompleted thoughts—any such breakdown in communications can hamstring the best-intentioned worker.

The Remedy: Close the communication gap. Make sure your instructions are crystal clear before you permit a person to get on with an assignment.

First, be sure you know what you want to say.

Second, say it clearly and concretely. Paint word pictures and form images that your subordinates can readily visualize, grasp, and understand.

Third, encourage questions. One of the costliest assumptions you can make is to believe that the absence of questions signifies perfect understanding. An employee may not ask any questions because he or she is uninterested in what you are saying, bored with how you are saying it, timid, daydreaming—the list could go on.

They Are Insufficiently Motivated. You don't scratch unless you itch. You don't sleep unless you are tired. You don't buy a newspaper unless you want to read about current events. You don't do *anything* without motivation. Before you perform any act, you must want or need to do it. And the act must fit the motive. Thus, you wouldn't hop into your car at midnight and drive twenty miles through a raging snowstorm to buy some cough drops. But you certainly would drive under these conditions if it were a question of rushing a sick child to a hospital.

The same holds true for winning employee cooperation. No employee is going to report for work at 5:30 A.M. because his boss wants to take advantage of daylight saving time. He might very well come in if he is informed that the company's biggest order of the year is at stake and he will be paid time and a half for the extra hours.

Frequently what appears to be employee uncooperativeness is really a case of insufficient motivation.

The Remedy: Make your subordinate want to do what you are asking him to do. Easier said than done? Perhaps. But there are techniques that work.

You can, for example, show him how he can realize an ambition of his own by cooperating with you. If he is looking for a promotion, you might point out that a cooperative spirit will be one of the factors considered when making recommendations.

You can appeal to his desire for approval. Everybody wants to be liked, complimented, appreciated. Convince your subordinate that what you want him to do will help him win approval in some way and you will kindle his interest. "The old man will be pleased to hear how you pitched in." "Here's an easy way to earn a reputation for dependability." "Your wife will be happy to learn that she's married to a real go-getter." These are just a few examples of appealing to the other person's desire for approval.

You can also harness his competitive instinct. Runners invariably perform better when they are pitted against other runners rather than against a stopwatch. Why? Because the very human desire to excel is best satisfied in live rivalry. A subordinate desires to turn out better work than his fellow employees. Just about everybody would like to improve on his own past performance. Explain how an individual can realize either of these ambitions by doing what you want and you will create the proper motivation for cooperation.

They Aren't Convinced that the Goal Is Important. Say "Do this!" to a group of employees and a certain number will unquestioningly do exactly what you want. A smaller number will think, "Sounds crazy, but if that's what you want, I'll do it." A still smaller number will think, "It's a senseless order, and I won't do it." Sometimes an employee is reluctant to cooperate because he remains unconvinced of the desirability, necessity, or value of the goal you have set for him. Either you have not explained why he ought to do as you say or you have explained it poorly.

The Remedy: Take whatever time is necessary to explain the thinking behind your instructions. If you suspect the existence of mental reservations in an employee, sincerely invite him to question you. So simple an observation as "You don't seem convinced. What's troubling you?" may be enough to extract whatever objection is on the employee's mind. Once you get it out of him, there are two possibilities: Either you will persuade him that the goal is worth working for, in which case you will gain his cooperation, or he will persuade you that it is not worth pursuing, in which case you will be prevented from making a mistake. Either way, you stand to gain.

Win Cooperation with the "Boomerang" Technique

If you are convinced that you are right, one approach you may be able to use is the boomerang technique: You take the employee's objection and, turning it around, use it as the very reason why she should do as you ask.

"I've never done that kind of job before," she protests.

"Exactly why you ought to jump at it," you reply. "It's a rare opportunity to gain added experience and round yourself out."

"The old way was better," she says.

"Sure it was—until now," you answer. "Just remember, there was a time when the old way was new and untried. Somebody like you tried it then and found that it worked better than the method it eventually replaced. That's called progress."

"Why give me the toughest project?" she moans.

Your answer? "The toughest project requires the best person. You're it, Sal."

Get the idea?

Use the boomerang technique whenever practical. It can be extremely effective.

The Importance of Feeling Important

You can take it as an axiom of effective management that people work with far more enthusiasm when they feel that someone is interested in them.

Most managers will readily concede that it is vital to make the people under them feel important, but they then blithely go on ignoring them. Result: Morale plunges, griping and absenteeism skyrocket, esprit de corps becomes nonexistent. Yet, it isn't all that difficult to boost a person's ego. Here are three techniques guaranteed to work.

Call Him by Name. H. C. Byrd, who coached the University of Maryland's football team for twenty-five years, used to tell of the tackle who always played his best game against Duke University on its home grounds. Why? Because Duke used a public address system in the stands. The tackle wanted to be in on every play so that he could hear his name blared out over the PA system between plays!

Napoleon boasted that he could call every one of his field officers by name. Franklin D. Roosevelt always repeated a stranger's name three times in the first three minutes of conversation in order to remember it. Conrad Hilton, whose success in the hotel field is legendary, insisted early in his career that every employee with logical access to a guest's name use it in addressing him.

Why should these men have gone out of their way to cultivate the habit of using people's names? Because they knew that it is one of the most powerful, convincing ways of saying, "I recognize you as an individual." So call your people by name. It doesn't cost you a cent; and it makes them feel like a million!

Pat Him on the Back. The person immune to the power of a sincere compliment has yet to be born. But make sure your compliment is true and well placed.

There is something praiseworthy about everyone. The field for the true compliment is limited only by your knowledge of an employee and your powers of observation. Has he recently handled a delicate situation with tact? Was his last report outstanding in one or more ways? Has he prevented you from committing an error? Is he particularly good at solving problems? Tell him so!

And, whenever possible, tell him in public.

Why?

Well, have you ever received a compliment in front of someone whose opinion you valued? Don't you feel extra special when you do? *That's* the power of public praise. Ever been pointed out by your boss to an outsider, then hear him say, "Meet one of our best men"? Remember how big you felt? That's the power of public praise.

You're no exception. Everybody gets a boot out of being brought to the attention of others. That's human nature. And every employee is human.

Show Respect for His Knowledge. In all probability, each individual you manage knows a lot more about his specialty than you do. Why not cash in on that know-how by asking his opinion in matters on which he is an authority? It's an unbeatable opportunity to show your respect for his knowledge and experience. In the process you will not only broaden your own horizons, you will give him the sweet satisfaction of having taught the boss.

There is also another advantage. The fact that you are not above listening to your people, but, endorse idea swapping by example, will encourage the kind of teamwork that gets things done.

Bringing Out the Best in Your People

Armed with an understanding of why employees behave as they do and what motivates them, you are now prepared for your primary responsibility, which is getting things done through the people who report to you.

How effectively you carry out that overriding responsibility determines the ultimate success of your company, your department, and yourself. Do your job well and you may anticipate increased production, high morale, and low employee turnover. Do it poorly and it is a foregone conclusion that output, morale, and sense of loyalty will sink.

Because there is a direct correlation between your own performance and that of your subordinates, your success as a manager depends on your ability to bring out the best in your people. You needn't threaten, shout, cajole, or browbeat them to get things done. You must simply learn to make them *want* to do their best.

That's what the effective manager does as a matter of course.

How can you do it?

In a variety of ways, depending on circumstances, personalities, and personal chemistry. However, there are several important guidelines you can follow.

Be Considerate. Nothing contributes more to building a strong, hardworking, loyal team than a considerate chief. He is courteous to subordinates. He puts himself in their place before making any decisions affecting them. He realizes that they have pride and self-respect and that by treating those characteristics as assets he will get much more effective work than he would by trampling on them.

Delegate Responsibility. This is the essence of administration. You are not a manager if you do not delegate, just as you are not a machinist if you cannot run a machine. The manager who insists on keeping his hand in details discourages his subordinates by competing with them. The capable employees will quit, the others will sit back and let him do the work. And the manager will have no time for his real job—thinking and planning.

Give Credit Where It Is Due. Taking credit for yourself that really belongs to one of your people destroys his initiative and willingness to take responsibility. Giving him proper recognition for what he does confers a double benefit: He gets credit for doing the job; you get credit for building an able team.

Show Interest in and Appreciation of Others. This is another way of saying, "Be a human being." Not all people are warmhearted by nature. But even the coldest-blooded manager can take steps to warm his relations with the people on his staff. For instance: Make occasional luncheon dates with one or two of your people at a time; find a way to mention hobbies, family news, or other not-too-personal matters; arrange informal bull sessions on business or nonbusiness topics. Interest is also shown by the boss who keeps a sharp eye on his people's work loads and similar matters. An occasional "Martha, you've been hitting the ball pretty hard lately. How about taking the afternoon off?" works wonders. Moves of this sort will pay dividends many times over in loyalty and accomplishment.

Set Goals for Your People. A good manager gives people a sense of direction, something to strive for and achieve because he or she understands that they need to know where they're going, what they're doing, and why they're doing it in order to plan their course intelligently and work efficiently.

Good employees can't get interested in working from day to day. So make the relationship between their day-to-day work and their larger goals clear. Don't, for example, stop with asking a person to study the operating costs of your department; explain that it's part of a plan to provide leeway for salary increases. And give your people information about your department, company, and industry so that they can see themselves and their work in perspective.

Don't Flex Your Muscle. It's far better to motivate employees to higher productivity than it is to drive them there. It isn't necessary to crack the whip to prove who is boss; there are better ways to encourage good work. Give employees target dates for assignments that might otherwise stretch out. Such goals will help give them an idea of the relative importance of various tasks.

Anticipate the Need for New Assignments. Many farsighted managers stockpile work assignments so that they will be ready when their employees complete current ones. If additional work isn't ready when employees are free to do it, something is wrong. If this is the case, check to see if the department is overstaffed. The situation might also be caused by some employees being overburdened while others do not have enough to do. Sometimes this occurs because work loads fluctuate from week to week; one answer is to hire temporary or part-time people for peak load periods.

Schedule Work Breathers. It's a good idea to set aside time for jobs that need doing, such as cleaning out files and maintaining records or reviewing procedures. Breathers should have a purpose, however, and should not stretch out or interfere with high-priority items.

Demonstrate Confidence in Your People. If you entertain any doubts about your department of staff, review them alone and in private. Exhibiting doubt to subordinates disheartens them and tends to destroy their confidence in you. If a leader is hesitant, how can he inspire his followers? Conversely, showing confidence builds others' self-confidence. Show by your words and deeds that you believe the work can be done and that you are confident of your people's ability to handle the job, and the work will get done.

Keep Them on Their Toes. Unfortunately, if employees can get away with mediocre work, that is precisely what a certain number of them will give you. It is up to you to help this minority reach out for the best they are capable of. You can do this by letting such employees know that you believe in their ability to turn out superior work and that you expect them to measure up to their responsibilities.

This approach presupposes that you know the intellectual capacities, physical stamina, and attitudes of your people, as well as their strengths and weaknesses, and that you give them assignments commensurate with their capabilities. If, under these circumstances, a person turns in shoddy work, you are justified in using the needle to spur him to improve. You must, of course, avoid demoralizing him or impairing his self-confidence in the process. But here are some perfectly allowable techniques.

• Return under-par work for redoing. Tell the employee what's wrong with the work and why you find it unacceptable. If he sees that he can't coast by, he'll get on the ball.
• Make him defend what he's done. If he thinks his work is acceptable, ask him how he went about it, what resources in or out of the company he used, how hard he worked, the extent to which he checked out his facts. Pin him down on details.
• Act promptly. Give him your criticism as soon as possible after the work is completed, though not before. Coaching is most effective when the job under discussion is fresh in both your minds.
• Criticize in private—for obvious reasons.

Tell Them What They're Doing Right. Most managers periodically sit down with their subordinates to let them know how they are doing on their jobs. More often than not, these appraisals tend to emphasize what's wrong and where improvement is needed. But don't overlook the importance of informing your people about what they're doing right, for the identification of a worker's achievements and strengths can be a most useful management tool.

For one thing, it helps motivate him. The more conscious a person is of what he has accomplished in the past, the more he is apt to attempt to accomplish in the future. By helping him identify past successes, you stimulate a worker to reach for his own top performance more of the time.

It gives him self-confidence too. Once he is led to face the pleasant fact that he has been capable of effort and success in the past, confidence in his own ability to duplicate, even surpass, those past efforts today will soar. He will dare more. And those who dare more, do more.

Admit Errors. Just as no employee expects his boss to be infallible, so no manager loses face when he admits he's wrong—if he isn't wrong too often! What you will gain is trust in your fairness and honesty, an asset beyond price to a manager.

Avoid "Demotivators"

While there is no precise antonym in English for *motivation,* the concept surely exists. Nor is it difficult to identify the phenomenon when it is present. People who work under its pall lack purpose, rarely demonstrate initiative, and are all too willing to settle for mediocre output.

A manager can have every personal factor in his favor—top wages, realistic goals, seasoned employees—but if he commits any of the following cardinal mistakes, he will critically injure his chances for motivating his people to better their performance. Indeed, he will be "demotivating" them.

Never Ignore What's Important to Your People. One of the best ways to find out what is uppermost in their minds, what the concerns and ambitions that move them are, is to encourage them to talk, to draw them out, to ask questions. Never dominate a conversation or a meeting, unless there is a good reason. In short, listen.

Never Have Too Many People Reporting to You. Many management theorists say that the optimum number of employees per manager is under ten. Rules of thumb are extremely handy, but broader averages can and are being used in today's organizations. For example, a group of new trainees or inexperienced employees requires more supervision than the same number of experienced and capable employees. Several factors affect the number of people you can effectively manage (and, therefore, successfully motivate): geographic dispersion, competence of employees, the complexity or repetitiveness of their work. If motivation, or its lack, is a problem, consider the possibility that you are simply spreading yourself too thin.

Never Allow Overlapping of Responsibilities. Franklin D. Roosevelt was famous for giving more than one man or organization the same mission, on the assumption that conflict and competition were good motivators.

And, for him, it mostly worked. But in times of national emergency governments can afford duplications of effort. Private enterprises seldom can. Having two or more people trying to do the same job is almost always an indication of poor organization. And if they know of the duplication in their assignments, they are apt to suspect that their manager doesn't trust them to go it alone. The inevitable result: "demotivation."

Never Overload. An ever-present danger is to overload a capable worker because he will get the job done with a minimum of fuss. But a wise manager recognizes that if you give even the best subordinate too many jobs and bog him down in details, his efficiency suffers. In the long run, a good worker is also apt to let such an experience affect his morale, and conceivably his motivation.

Never Take Anything for Granted. Nor should you assume that employees understand their assignments simply because you explained them once. Periodically review the work of all employees to make sure they have the same understanding of their duties that you have.

Never Set a Bad Example. There has never been a successful manager, one who could motivate the people under him, who himself was not highly motivated. The best motivators are those who are hardworking themselves, for you motivate largely by example. Despite the hostility behind statements that employees sometimes make about hardworking, dedicated superiors, there is always a sense of pride as well. Employees like to feel that they are living up to an image of their boss, particularly when the boss is devoted to the job of making his or her company successful.

Never Belittle Subordinates. No person likes to think that others regard him as stupid or incompetent. He may have doubts of his own, but he doesn't like others agreeing with him. Generally, you can reprimand an employee using other terms—*lax, lazy, indifferent, sloppy*—but call him *stupid* and you will rapidly destroy his initiative. This term flattens most people. After all, how can a person throw himself into his work when he's just been labeled a loser?

Never Stint on Equipment. Few things frustrate an employee more surely than to be assigned a job and then be given inadequate equipment for it. For example, if your budget makes it impossible to provide a dictating machine for everyone who needs one, then allow for this in your performance standards or revamp assignments so that fewer people need to use the machine.

Never Stifle Initiative. Let your people solve their own problems and you will have gone a long way toward helping yourself and your company as well. For example, have you taught them to tackle a difficulty by asking, "What's the problem?" rather than stating, "We're in trouble"? Do they understand that the problem should be stated specifically—that "We have a cost problem" is wrong, whereas "We must cut expenses by at least 8 percent" is correct? Do they all know where to get help for different problems? And do you encourage them to stick with a problem no matter how tough it may be—and to look for new approaches?

Never Be Hard to See. Some managers believe that a certain inaccessibility is the mark of a true leader. A few even think it is a status symbol. They couldn't be more wrong. When someone who works for you wants to talk, it's only good management to make yourself available promptly, because effective leaders have to know what's happening around them. Problems shouldn't have to reach the crisis stage before you hear about them. No matter what the demands on your time may be, no matter how much paper work or how many other obligations you may have, there is no excuse for not knowing what's going on.

The best source of information, and one for which there is no substitute, is the people who report to you. If they know you are interested in what they are doing, and if you give them a chance, they'll gladly talk. But if you are impatient, disinterested, hard to get to, overly critical, or your attention wanders, nobody is going to consult you about anything until he or she absolutely has to.

Astute managers make it easy for subordinates to get through to them. People don't have to request formal interviews every time they want to talk to them. These leaders make themselves accessible, and they listen.

Furthermore, they don't become openly irritated if the news isn't good. We all prefer good news to bad; that's human. But if people find their bosses getting sore when things aren't going right, they are reluctant to let them know when there's trouble. And that usually only serves to aggravate the situation. In the end, they and their boss find themselves battling one crisis after another, a situation that virtually guarantees the death of morale and motivation.

Never Let Emotions Get the Upper Hand.   No matter how temporarily comforting it may be, it seldom pays to get angry. An angry person is, momentarily, a foolish person. Emotion blocks out logic. If he is frequently angry, he is also apt to be a sick person. Continued anger takes a heavy toll on mind and body.

Why, then, do we keep on doing it? Probably because it's natural, instinctive, and briefly satisfying. And because we haven't stopped to realize how harmful it is.

Yet, that's exactly what a successful manager must do. He can't afford the luxury of a temper that makes him say and do foolish things and sours his relationship with his people.

The most important time to hold your temper is when the other fellow has lost his. It takes two to tangle. When someone else starts to grow angry, make it a point never to respond in kind, no matter what the temptation. To be sure, this will sometimes require a Herculean effort on your part, but the payoff is worth the effort: Nothing to be sorry for, nothing to apologize for, no strained relations to mend, and the respect of your people.

The individual who unremittingly seeks ways in which to increase his knowledge, productivity, and creativity usually succeeds, for he is announcing in the most convincing way possible—demonstration—that he is willing to pay the price of advancement. You have taken a giant step toward promotion be reading *Moving On Up*. If it has done its job, this book has increased your understanding of your true potential and helped you discern the many areas in which that potential may be realized.

But life, unlike books, doesn't come in neat chapters. Every achievement is inevitably accompanied by new challenges, and promotions are no exception. Consequently, now that you've climbed the next rung of the ladder, what should you be prepared for?

13

So You've Been Promoted —Now What?

"Congratulations! You've been promoted."

Sweet music though these words may be, they are often the prelude to a hornet's nest of anxieties, personality clashes, and assorted problems.

Perhaps the toughest part of being promoted is handling the new relationships the change in status creates. There you are, up one rung of the ladder, and suddenly the people alongside whom you've been working as equals find themselves reporting to you. The results may range from awkward to disastrous, for working against you are a host of understandably human emotions—such as envy, suspicion, and fear.

There will be some who are genuinely happy for you, who perceive your advancement as corroboration of the fact that hard work, talent, and dedication are rewarded. But not every single one of your colleagues is likely to take so sanguine a view of your success.

How do you handle such a situation? What can you say—what can you do—to ease things for yourself and for those you now manage? There is probably no one correct strategy, because every person and situation is different. But there are certain general principles, adherence to which should help smooth the transition period.

Recognize That You Have a Few Things Going for You. For one thing, unless the promotion also involves a transfer to another department, you are in the enviable position of knowing your people—their weaknesses, their strengths, their pet peeves, their ambitions, what makes them tick. For another, barring only extreme introversion on your part, you probably have the additional advantage of being able to communicate with them. You're on a first-name basis with them. You can talk, and be talked to, freely. Both are extremely important. Finally, assuming that you deserved your promotion, you should have their respect, whether or not it is grudgingly given.

Don't Apologize for Your New Position. You've earned your promo-

166

tion. Remember that. Management must have decided that, of all likely candidates, you were the best qualified. So accept your promotion. Any uncertainty or air of apology on your part puts you on the defensive—a bad posture for any manager and potentially fatal for a new one.

Face the Situation Openly.   Depending on your relationship with each of your people, sit down with them either individually or collectively and verbalize what is on your mind: Tell them that your altered relationship is as new for you as it is for them, but it's a fact of life. You are now their manager. There is no reason why it should adversely affect the performance of either any individual or the department as a whole. To the contrary, you might point out, there are distinct advantages to being managed by "one of their own"—you know their problems, their abilities, and their work loads; and you speak their language. Ask for their cooperation. People usually enjoy being asked for help and tend to respond positively.

Give Them a Sense of Participation.   All beginnings present opportunities. As a new manager, you are in a position to correct any inequities that may exist in the way your department is currently organized or run. This is a good time to poll your people, to find out what's on their minds, to determine if they have any ideas on how such things as work loads or work flow can be improved. Most employees have ideas—some good, some bad, but all worth listening to. You'll learn and, maybe, experience your first success as a manager—getting things running better. People like to have a say in their own destinies. If you encourage them to take part in your decision-making process, they will recognize what you are trying to do and in all likelihood, will cooperate.

Remember What You Wanted Yesterday.   Don't let your promotion go to your head. It wasn't so long ago that you wanted to be told the reasons behind your assignment, thirsted for a word of encouragement and praise, liked consistent and predictable supervision, enjoyed working for someone you could respect. Remember what you wanted in a manager yesterday and you will have a reliable guide to what your people expect from you today.

Learn from Your Former Manager's Mistakes.   As good as he may have been, he probably had some failings, shortcomings that were easier to spot as an employee than as a fellow manager. Take stock of what they were and try not to repeat them. If, for example, he was secretive and noncommunicative, do what you can to be open and aboveboard with your people. If he held the reins too tightly, don't continue that policy. Admittedly, some distasteful practices may have to be retained, such as when a lazy employee needs periodic prodding to perform, but there is no reason to do anything just because your predecessor did it that way. One of your responsibilities as a manager now is to seek, and find, better ways to get things done. So do it, but do it your way if it is more efficacious.

Make It Your Business to Learn the Ropes.   One way to earn the respect of your people is to become a reliable source of company information. How, for example, does the company's new dental plan work? What's the current policy on salary increases? To whom can they go if there is an error in their paychecks? How can they enroll for a company-run course? As a manager, you're expected either to have the answers to such questions or to know where they can be obtained.

Study Up on Management Skills.   Most promotions tend to be given to people who excel in their jobs rather than to those who have any special gift for human relations. Yet the job of managing requires certain skills that even the best worker may not necessarily possess—tact and the ability to inspire loyalty, for example. If you recognize that you lack any of the generally accepted management skills, start your own self-development program. Read a few good books on the subject. Reread the sections of this book that deal with being an effective, successful manager. If possible, enroll in a course in basic management. And if yours is one of the companies that offer in-house courses on the subject, take advantage of it.

Give Recognition.   Few things turn employees off faster or more enduringly than the manager who is a "glory hog." You like to receive credit for your ideas. So do your people. Be quick, therefore, to show appreciation for good work and see to it that individuals receive the proper acknowledgment for their contributions, whether it takes the form of a prize, bonus, raise, or a simple public expression of gratitude. Such rewards are not only deserved; they are extremely practical. Recognition tends to raise employee standards as well as morale. Next time they'll try to equal or surpass the good job they did this time. And those who witness the recognition will be spurred on to greater effort. A little friendly competition never hurt anyone.

Learn To Say No. Perhaps the most uncomfortable situation a newly promoted manager confronts is the one that requires him, in all good conscience, to turn down a former peer's suggestion or request. By reacting negatively, he risks giving the impression that his recently conferred authority has gone to his head. Yet, he cannot accede to ideas in which he sees no merit simply in order to be a "regular" guy. It can be a dilemma.

So there you are, forced to say no. How should you do it?

In a word, tactfully.

Here are some responses that have worked for others. They may work for you.

• "My hands are tied." It's contrary to company policy . . . your boss's orders . . . government regulations. You've made a previous, conflicting commitment. You would get into some kind of hot water if you did.

• "It doesn't fall under my jurisdiction." You lack the authority to say yes.

• "Put yourself in my place." By drawing an analogy between what the other person is asking you to do and a similarly unreasonable request that a third party might make of him or her, you can frequently get off the hook on the basis of simple justice.

• "It would set a bad precedent." You can't afford to make any exceptions because of the chain reaction it would trigger.

• "I have a better suggestion." If you can, offer an alternative to the request that you *are* able to perform. Or show him a way out that he can take himself. Or steer him to somebody who you think might be in a better position to help. (But be very sure that, in the process, you aren't putting the third party on the spot.)

Avoid Dangerous Management Traps. It's normal to take pride in a promotion, but it can also be a temptation to throw your weight around, settle old scores, and forget some of the niceties that make for good human relations. Obviously, no one who did all these things would be promoted in the first place, but some managers, particularly new ones, occasionally fall into one or another of these bad practices. Keep your guard up against them at all times.

Don't Ignore Your People. You needn't devote every waking moment to your employees, but from time to time it is important to give your undivided, individual attention to every person under your direct control. Periodically invite each one into your office; there, in privacy, give him your complete attention. Let him know you care about him. Don't let the telephone disturb you; don't let your secretary or anyone else interrupt. If you do, the employee will feel that there is probably no occasion when he can hold your undivided attention.

Don't Become Constantly Preoccupied with Your Own Interests. First things first, right? In this case, wrong! Of course your own future is your primary concern, but there is no need to broadcast this to others. You don't want them to think that you are selfish, that you are manipulating them for your own purposes. For example, don't ask your secretary or assistant to stay late finishing a job only so that *you* can impress others tomorrow; allow him to share the credit.

Don't Embarrass a Weak Performer. Don't show off at the expense of a subordinate—for instance, by doing a particular job better or faster than he can do it himself. It's important to every human being's dignity to be able to do something well on his own, and when you take his work away, you also take away his self-respect. You are, in short, demotivating him. On the other hand, tolerating the efforts of weak or inefficient personnel can utterly destroy the initiative of the best people in your department. If you find that a worker can't perform well, therefore, don't embarrass him. But don't tolerate him, either. If he can't be trained, discharge him and get someone else to do the job the way you want it done.

Don't Be Indecisive. It is a sign of strength to be able to make decisions promptly and wisely. If you lack confidence, if you are afraid to stick your neck out, you will infect your people with the same kind of uncertainty. Add indecision to any of the previous mistakes and your whole motivation effort will crumble around you.

Don't Be Erratic. The poor manager, typically, is mindful of other people's feelings one day and flies off the handle at the slightest provocation on another. Once employees consider you unpredictable, they will deny you their confidence as well as their cooperation, both of which you must have in order to get your job done. People only follow the leader whose course is steady and whose actions are predictable.

Don't Be Secretive. As members of a team, your workers are entitled to know what's going on. You needn't burden them with changes in policy and problems that aren't their immediate concern. But they should know enough about conditions and events in your company and industry to see themselves and their jobs in perspective. As a result they will be more likely to accept your instructions, suggestions, and orders.

Don't Be Stingy with Your Praise. Properly handled, praise can be one of the most important motivators in management's arsenal. It is especially helpful when you praise someone in the area of his deepest anxiety, where he is trying to do a good job and where you know he feels he ought to be making some progress. It's also a good policy to save your praise for a particularly difficult job that is handled with special distinction.

It would seem the easiest thing in the world to pat a person on the back. But there is more to praising someone than meets the eye. For maximum results, make your praise meaningful in terms of the employee's performance and avoid superlatives, for few workers will swallow obvious flattery. An unadorned but sincere "Good work" is far more effective than puffery. But don't be miserly either. Although too-frequent praise can become meaningless, praise doled out reluctantly hurts morale. If a man is doing his level best and comes through in a pinch—even if unspectacularly—let him know that his efforts are appreciated. It will pay off in improved performance.

Don't Lose Your Sense of Priorities. Every order you issue cannot possibly carry the same weight of urgency. Employees soon catch on to the manager to whom everything has top priority. Like the villagers who ignored the boy who cried "Wolf!" too often, they will cease to take you seriously.

Don't Make a Fuss over Your Promotion. By protesting too much about how you are still "one of the boys," you may plant the seeds of suspicion where none existed before. Clearly, you should avoid giving your people any reason for suspecting that your promotion has gone to your head.

Go About Your Business. The final rule. You were promoted to do a job. Do it. The sooner you settle into the new routine, the sooner your people will too.

No one can anticipate all the problems that a promotion may trigger, to be sure. Certainly, there are many more than just the new relationship created between the manager and his or her people. But that new relationship is one of the most crucial in terms of a department's productivity. If you fail to imbue the people reporting to you with a spirit of cooperation and dedication to mutual goals, you may find your promotion assuming the dimensions of a burden instead of what, ideally, it ought to be: an exciting opportunity to test your own potential, to see how far up the ladder you can go. But if, like most successful people, you discover that you are more than equal to the challenge, it won't be long before you find yourself setting your sights higher . . . and higher . . . and higher.

You may even want to reread this book.

We have covered several hundred specific ways to make yourself worthy of advancement, ranging from increasing your personal output to motivating those under you. It would be unrealistic to expect any individual to practice every single technique discussed. Some may not apply to your current situation or responsibility. That's all right.

The important thing is to be aware of all the separate traits, habits, and techniques that, in combination, contribute to the makeup of a comer. As you go through your workday, bear in mind the many ways in which you can improve. If you cannot use all the techniques here, don't grow discouraged. Try one or two. As you gain confidence in your ability to change your ways and do your work more effectively, you will be encouraged to try a third and fourth. And so on.

Self-improvement is never easy. It requires great honesty with oneself, a lot of time, a burning desire to succeed, discipline, and perseverance. But through steady progress, no matter how small at first, you can ultimately transform yourself into the person you want to be. For the simple and encouraging truth is that *you* control your future.

Index

Ability, importance of, 19
Accomplishment, sense of, 27–28
Accuracy, concentration on, 45–46
Admitting errors, 56
Aggression, 42
American Telephone and Telegraph Company, 21
Appearance, 41
Appreciation of others, 159
Aristotle, 140
Asking effective questions, 54–55
Assignment
  organizing, 50–51
  seeing opportunity in, 50
Atlas, Charles, 43
Attention to little things, 27–28
Attitude and confidence, 41–42

Bad work habits, 72–73
Barnum, Phineas Taylor, 18
Bell, Alexander Graham, 19
Bell, Marcus, 22
Bethlehem Steel Corporation, 22
Bettger, Frank, 30
Body temperature, personal productivity and, 75–76
Boomerang technique, 156
Boredom, 73
Bosses' errors, learning from, 26
Brady, Diamond Jim, 18–19
Brains, picking others, 51
Breakfast, 74
Breaks, taking, 87–88

Business letters, writing better, 104–105
Byrd, H. C., 157

Carlyle, Thomas, 23
Carnegie, Andrew, 23
Carpentier (boxer), 59
Chaucer, Geoffrey, 46
Churchill, Sir Winston, 43, 87
Clear oral messages, 95–96
Clutter, getting rid of, 65
Coffee break, 86, 87–88
Communication skills, 92–112
  clear speaking, 95–96
  diction, 94–95
  in the meeting room, 107–112
  speech, 98–103
  talking way to success, 92–93
  vocabulary, 96–98
  voice, 93–94
  writing, 103–107
Competitors' errors, learning from, 26–27
Completing a job, 27
Concentration, 82–85
  benefits of, 83
  letting interest take over, 84–85
  tuning out the world, 83–84
Confidence, demonstrating (in others), 160
Confidence killers (and antidote), 30–34
  ego-shaking experience, 31
  excessive humility, 34

Confidence killers (*cont.*)
  failure, 31
  false assumptions, 32
  formal education lack, 32–33
  illness, 33–34
  lack of job knowledge, 34
  laziness, 33
  pessimistic friends, 33
  worry, 31–32
Consideration, 159
Cooperation, dealing with people
      and, 154–156
  boomerang technique, 156
  employee uncooperativeness,
      154–156
"Core" activities, 64
Creativity, 139–149
  climate for, 143–144
  how people tick, 140–143
  managing creative people,
      144–149
  meaning of, 139–140
Credit, giving (to others when
      due), 159
Criticism, accepting, 23–24
Cultivating a habit, 57–61
Curie, Marie, 141
Curiosity, 141

Darrow, Clarence, 131
Deadlines, 77–78
Decisiveness, 88
Delegation (learning and avoiding
      traps), 80–82
  avoiding traps, 81–82
  beneath potential, 82
  commensurate authority, 82
  communicating effectively, 81–
      82
  learning, 80–81
  not allowing for error, 82
  not enough, 81
Demonstration
  sales, 128–129
  teaching, 119

"Demotivators," avoiding, 162–
      165
Dempsey, Jack, 59
Dependability, 28
Descartes, René, 140
Diction, 94–95
Disagreeing, learning how, 24–25
Discouragement, 73–74
Drive, 141

Easy-to-hear words, using, 95–96
Eating-alone time, 70
Edison, Thomas, 141, 143
Education lack, antidote for, 32–
      33
Efficiency-improving techniques,
      86
Ego-shaking experience, antidote
      for, 31
Einstein, Albert, 141, 142
Employee goals, setting, 159–160
Enthusiasm
  developing, 37–38
  when teaching, 116
Errors, admitting, 162
Evenings, making time for, 69–
      70
Excellence, habit of, 55
Experts' testimony, sales, and,
      129–130
Explosive confrontations, de-
      fusing, 24–25
Extra time, where to find, 69–71

Failure, antidote for, 31
False assumption, antidote for,
      32
Fear, 38–41
  conquering physical expressions
      of, 40–41
  and how to sell ideas, 135–136
  mastering, 38–39
  as reaction to unknown situa-
      tion, 39

Feeling important, importance of, 157–158
Flexibility, 49, 53, 57
Forbes (magazine), 27
Ford, Henry, 139
Formalities, skipping, 67
Form letters, 68
Fortune (magazine), 27
Friends' errors, learning from, 26
Freud, Sigmund, 141
Future accomplishment, foundation for, 87

Gates, Bet-A-Million, 19
Generalities, avoiding, 96
General principles, looking for, 46–47
Getting up earlier, 69

Half-hour meetings, 65
Harmful attitudes, 73–74
Hilton, Conrad, 157
Hoarding ideas, habit of, 51
Holidays, making time for, 70
Humility, excessive, antidote for, 34
Humor, sense of, 143

Ideas, how to sell, 123–138
  asking for the order, 131
  backing up promises with evidence, 128–130
  both sides of story strategy, 133–134
  climax versus anticlimax orders, 133
  defining the idea, 124–125
  by demonstrating belief, 126–128
  to different people, 137–138
  establishing a deadline, 130–131
  fear and, 135–136
  fighting inertia, 131–133
  letting listener draw conclusions, 134

Ideas, how to sell, (*cont.*)
  letting listener talk, 136–137
  "product" and prospect's psyche, 125–126
  repetition and, 137
  as salespeople, 123
  when to admit limitations, 134
Idiosyncrasy, 143
Ignorance, admitting, 114
Illinois Central Railroad, 21–22
Illness, antidote for, 33–34
Imagination, 142
Impulsive decisions, 56
Indecision, 73
Inferiority feelings, reasons for, 42
Intuition, 142–143

James, William, 40, 60–61
Jefferson, Thomas, 140
Job analysis, 12–14
  eliminating weaknesses, 13–14
Job knowledge lack, antidote for, 34
Job operation, knowing in entirety, 20–21

Keeping a promise, 27
Kerr, Jean, 83
Kettering, Charles, 142
Knowledge, respect for (in others), 158

Langmuir, Irving, 142–143
Law of association, 47
Law of contrast, 48
Law of similarity, 48
Law of succession, 47–48
Laziness, antidote for, 33
Learning habits, how to cultivate, 44–48
  building on what you know, 48
  concentration on accuracy, 45–46
  general principles for, 46–47
  intention to learn, 45

Learning habits, how to cultivate (*cont.*)
  and overlearning, 48–49
  seeking to understand, 46
Learning process, 14–15
  to disagree, 24–25
  from mistakes of others, 25–27
Lincoln, Abraham, 29, 30
Logical thinking, 55–56
Long-winded visitors, 67–68

Mails, using, 69
Managerial ability, 17
Markham, Charles, 21–22
Mediocrity, 73
  how to avoid (in an employee), 161
Meeting room communication, 107–112
  conducting the discussion, 109–110
  finishing up, 110–111
  getting the discussion rolling, 109
  post-meeting factor, 111–112
  presenting the problem, 108–109
Meetings, limiting time for, 65
Memorizing, 85
Memos, writing, 105–106
Merton, R. K., 126
Michaelangelo, 139
Minor decisions, anticipating, 74
Mistake insurance, 88–89
Murray, Arthur, 43

Napoleon I, 157
New assignments, anticipating need for, 160
Newton, Issac, 43

Observation, 142
Olivier, Laurence, 139
Opportunity, importance of, 19

Overcompensation, 42
Overlearning, 48–49

People, dealing with creatively, 150–165
  avoiding "demotivators," 162–165
  bringing out the best, 158–162
  cooperation and, 154–156
  employee desires and motivation, 150–151
  importance of feeling important, 157–158
  self-image and, 153–154
  what employees want, 151–153
Perseverance, 141
Pessimistic friends, antidote for, 33
Physical inventory, 75
Planning strategy, 11–17
  choosing successor, 17
  commonsense precautions, 11–12
  decision for promotion, 15–16
  eliminating weaknesses, 13–14
  job analysis, 12–14
  lack of, 73
  learning process, 14–15
Plato, 140
Points, making one at a time, 96
Pope, Alexander, 43
Posture, 86
Practice, 121
Precise words, using, 49
Priorities
  checking, 80
  setting, 76
Procrastination, 72–73
"Procrastination drawer," 86–87
Productivity, personal, 72–91
  bad work habits and, 72–73
  body temperature and, 75–76
  concentration, 82–85
  decisiveness, 88

Productivity, personal (*cont.*)
  delegation, 80–82
  efficiency-improving techniques,
    86
  establishing time limits, 76–77
  for future accomplishment, 87
  getting the job done, 78–79
  harmful attitudes, 73–74
  learning to stop work, 90–91
  mistake insurance, 88–89
  physical inventory, 75
  posture, 86
  priorities, 76, 80
  problems without immediate
    solutions, 91
  "procrastination drawer," 86–
    87
  realistic deadlines, 77–78
  reducing work load, 89–90
  starting the day right, 74
  taking a break, 87–88
  thirty-day cycle, 79–80
  when to memorize, 85
Progress, big job, 78–79
"Promotability," characteristics
  of, 21–22
Promotion
  decision for, 15–16
  how to handle, 166–172
  and successor, 17
Psychology Department (Columbia University), 78–79
Public relations program, 18–28
  accepting criticism, 23–24
  attention, paying (to little
    things), 27–28
  being a maverick, 22–23
  knowing the job, 20–21
  learning to disagree, 24–25
  learning from mistakes of
    others, 25–27
  making others aware, 20
  "promotability," 21–22
  recognition, 18–20

Pulitzer, Joseph, 29, 30
Punctuality, 28

Rapidly, working, 65
Rationalization, 42
Reading time, 68
Recognition, importance of, 18–
  20
Reflex habit, 73
Regression, 42
Repetition, teaching, 120
Report writing, 106–107
Responsibility, delegating, 159
Ripley, Robert, 62
Rock Island Railroad, 22
Rogers, Will, 34
Roosevelt, Franklin D., 157
Roosevelt, Theodore, 22

St. Louis Post-Dispatch, 29
Scarne, John, viii
Schedule, 53, 67
  and work breather, 160
Schwab, Charles, 22
Self-confidence, 28, 29–43, 142,
    161–162
  appearance, 41
  attitude, 41–42
  determining strengths and
    weaknesses, 35–36
  developing enthusiasm, 37–38
  fear and, 38–41
  image, 42–43
  knowing the job, 35
  lack and antidote for, 30–34
  self-development plan, 36–37
Self-image
  and confidence, 42–43
  and dealing with people, 153–
    154
  questionnaire, 1–10
Self-motivation, lack of, 74
Sensitivity, when teaching, 116–
    117

Shakespeare, William, 141
Shortcuts, habit of looking for, 50
Short letters, writing, 65
Simple words, using, 95
Simpson, O. J., 43
Sims, William Snowden, 23
Socrates, 19
Speaking wisely, 27
Speech making, 98–103
  the closing, 101
  getting material together, 99
  making an outline, 99–100
  miscellaneous tips, 102–103
  the opening, 100–101
  pause and opening remarks,
    101–102
Standing, when unannounced
    visitors drop by, 64
Statistics, sales, 130
Stopping work effectively, learn-
    ing how, 90–91
Strategy for getting ahead
  dealing with people, 15–165
  handling a promotion, 166–172
  managing creativity, 139–149
  personal productivity, 72–91
  planning, 11–17
  public relations, 18–28
  self-confidence, 29–43
  selling ideas, 123–138
  teachers and teaching, 113–122
  time, 62–71
  winning habits, 44–61
Strengths
  determining, 35–36
  job analysis, 13
  turning weaknesses into, 13–14
Subgoals
  establishing, 51–53
  getting a big job done, 78–79
Subordinates' errors, learning
    from, 26

Talking it over, 50
Teachers and teaching, 113–122

Teachers and teaching (*cont.*)
  accentuating the positive, 119–
    120
  breaking down material, 117–
    118
  demonstration, 119
  enthusiasm, 116
  getting instructions across, 114
  with honesty, 114
  knowing the material, 113–114
  in logical sequence, 118–119
  and making points stick, 121–
    122
  organizing the presentation, 115
  practice, 121
  proficiency, 113
  and repetition, 120
  sensitivity, 116–117
  tools, 115–116
  up-to-date facts, 114
  whole picture (before filling
    in details), 117
Telephone conversations, keeping
    short, 64
Thinking habit, 49–50
  flexibility, 49
  precise words, 49
  taking time, 50
  talking it over, 50
Thirty-day cycle (habit), 79–80
Time, making, 62–71
  checking yourself, 63
  "core" activities, 64
  and critical assessment, 50
  extra time, 69–71
  fifty-seven-week year and,
    62–63
  getting rid of clutter, 65
  keeping in the present, 66
  long-winded callers and, 67–68
  reading time, 68
  skipping formalities, 67
  starting day off right, 74
  time estimate costs, 66–67
  trimming the workday, 64–65

Time, making (*cont.*)
    using form letters, 68
    using the mails, 69
Time limits, establishing, 76–77
Travel time, 70
Truman, Harry, 87
Tunney, Gene, 60`
20/20 listening, 53–54

Understand, seeking to, 46

Vail, Theodore, 21
Visual evidence, sales and, 128
Vocabulary, 96–98
    tips on how to add power to,
        97–98
Voice communication, 93–94
    bending, 93
    loudness, 93–94
    pitch, 94
    speed, 93
Voltaire, 43

Waiting time, 70
Wall Street Journal, The, 27
Weakness
    determining, 35–36
    eliminating, 13–14

Weekdays, making time for, 70
Winning habits, how to cultivate,
        44–61
    admitting errors, 56
    asking effective questions, 54–
        55
    excellence, 55
    flexibility, 57
    habit, 57–61
    hoarding ideas, 51
    learning, 44–49
    logical thinking, 55–56
    shortcuts, 50–51
    subgoals, 51–53
    thinking, 49–50
    20/20 listening, 53–54
Worker errors, learning from, 26
Work load, ways to reduce, 89–90
Worry, antidote for, 31–32
Writing, 103–107
    better business letters, 104–105
    with impact, 103–104
    memos, 105–106
    reports, 106–107

Xanthippe, 19